CHA$ING TWENTIE$

Getting into a Tool Truck Business

Chasing Twenties Rick Murray Published by Richard murray, 2020. While every precaution has been taken in the preparation of this book, the publisher assumes no responsibility for errors or omissions, or for damages resulting from the use of the information contained herein.

CHASING TWENTIES

First edition. October 25, 2020.

Copyright © 2020 Rick Murray.

ISBN: 978-0-578-79819-6

Written by Rick Murray.

TABLE OF CONTENT$

- **Introduction**
- **Chapter One**
- **Chapter Two**
- **Chapter Three**
- **Chapter Four**
- **Chapter Five**
- **Chapter Six**
- **Chapter Seven**
- **Chapter Eight**
- **Chapter Nine**
- **Chapter Ten**
- **In Closing**

By Rick Murray

To my beautiful wife that puts up with all the work. My family and friends support me each step of the way. Making this possible!

Introduction

WHO AM I, AND WHAT right do I have to tell you anything about the tool truck industry? Let's start at the beginning on who I am and where I came from. My name is Rick Murray. I was born in 1981 in Altoona, PA, to two government-employed conservative parents. I grew up in Pennsylvania with two little brothers. Believe me when I say there was nothing special about us - but we developed an obsession with tinkering on go-karts and motorcycles as much as possible at an early age. We were always begging to get more stuff to work on, and more tools of course. This would be the start of my tool addiction.

I started wrestling in junior high school and continued through college. Wrestling played a big role in my life. You see, I was a punk kid that didn't know much of anything, and the public school system decided I had a learning disability. That was just a politically correct way of saying "lazy." Whatever the reason, I found reading incredibly difficult. When I was growing up, I felt like there were four TV screens turned on at one time in my head. I just had to get the patience to read, and reread subjects, to learn them. Not a thing a punk kid wants to do, especially growing up. So, I joined wrestling instead.

Wrestling was like a calamitous addiction and, in general, isn't a pleasant sport to do. But it helped me then and it helped me later in the tool truck business. You see, when I call it a calamitous addiction, I don't mean it like drugs or alcohol. I mean it in a way that it's just you out there, one-on-one against your opponent. No help is coming in the middle of battle. Short of screaming for a coach (like your franchisor in the tool business), it's all you that makes it happen. The point is, this sport helped my learning-disabled mind conceptualize the key components in my life. Here are a few lessons wrestling taught me, and how I applied them to my business:

1. Hard work does pay off eventually, and it does so in ways that you never knew could happen.

2. Time devotion, giving your sport or business the required time, is essential. Not just punching a clock but prioritizing and maximizing each hour, minute, and second so that you're giving everything you have to move forward in your ultimate quest.

3. Patience to deal with some of the most adverse situations and people you will ever deal with in your life. This will push you to your limit and then continue to push you well past your accepted limit, having the confidence in yourself to overcome the many obstacles that will be presented.

4. Determination and persistence in sport and business, means you can never quit, even after a failure. Getting knocked down is not a "maybe." Getting right back up after the worst beatings will make your success to some degree in this business—at least, it did for me!

Do you need to be a wrestler to succeed in this business? Not at all! Do you need grit and determination? Definitely!

Now, remember my brothers and I were somewhat mechanically inclined growing up. We always loved motorsports and playing with whatever we could get our hands on. Between the seasons of wrestling in the frozen Pennsylvania winters, we did our best with the crappy bikes being stitched together to ride moto-cross from the spring to summer months. We all had a passion - which remains even to this day, to different degrees - for riding on two wheels. To be able to do this, we had to work on our own stuff since our parents never purchased bikes for us. At the primitive stage, I can remember that with no money or parental money, but with a drive to go fast, came the need for tools to fix our bikes. From the Craftsman starter tools to the major professional tool lines, we learned quickly the value of good tools and how hard it is to acquire them. Like a cute girl at a bar winking at you, the attraction begins.

The years of amateur moto-cross racing and the love of working on the bikes led to a small motorcycle repair shop. At first, we operated out of our parents' garage, then moved into a larger place. Still a mixture of semi-hobby and semi-serious, we made some money on repairs for other people and bikes that we fixed and flipped.

By this time, we were getting older and starting to get jobs or careers outside of the repair shop. Working to me was like a slow death march with a tyrant boss that controls your pay, time, and right to grow. They do this to you weekly, daily, hourly for that paycheck. This is where I found my drive, or maybe you found your drive, to look for more in life, to use your skills to get out of the tyrant's oppression. In my case, it was hatred. I've got nothing against jobs and bosses, I just don't have the drive to please them. Occasionally in life you get those bosses that you despise so much it pushes you to the next level. Maybe you have one and you're here with me! I know I was lucky enough to have more than one. Lucky you, you might say?

At one stage, I was living in Harrisburg, PA, where I spent a couple of years working as a copier repair technician. I was living a pretty normal life as a married homeowner. I still worked on my bikes and my customers' bikes with my brothers. The main issue was that I had these things called GOALS! With the goals came expectations that I had for myself. Not obtaining my goals, or even trying, was eating me up inside. You see, one of my biggest role models was this guy named Mike Strollo. This man had several successful businesses in the rural parts of Pennsylvania outside Pittsburgh. I'd spend some time in the summers as a child visiting him and his businesses, and get odd jobs from him cleaning up. One of his businesses was a hardware store and another was a carpet store. This man was my grandfather. He supplied my extended family work and income through the businesses. He was one of the baddest dudes on the planet to me when I was growing up. Has there been someone in your life that you looked up to running their own business, and gave you the entrepreneur's impact? I got the inspiration from Grandpa Mike.

So here I am, twenty-seven years old, having a conversation with my good friend over some beers about how unhappy I am with work, PA life and its brutally cold temperatures, and overall frustration of not achieving my goals of being a business owner in a place where I want to live. If this sounds familiar to you, you're not alone. I'm super lucky that I had a good enough friend to shoot it to me straight, and I quote: "If you're unhappy then get the heck up and change it, go after what you want in life." I took his advice to heart and it felt like a match had been lit to start the fire! I needed to stop making excuses and *change my life*!

So, with the right plans (or the best plans I could come up with), I sold my home and all of my possessions (except some haulable tools), loaded up my pickup truck and headed for California. Why California? We'd visited the state a few years prior, travelling from San Francisco to San Diego. I fell in love with San Diego. That was where I wanted to be. After packing up and selling almost everything, the wife and I headed west. After two weeks on the road, including a stopover to visit my little brother living in San Antonio, Texas, we landed in San Diego. Even now, I find it one of the most beautiful places I've ever seen. My mindset at that time was to put it all on the line and fulfil my dream of self-ownership, and this is where I wanted to do it. If I went down in flames, at least I was going to do it somewhere that I wanted to be.

I needed to get set up in San Diego with a home and income stream, and to learn the lay of the land. I did this over the next few months, finding an affordable home and the same employment I had in PA as a copier tech. With roots planted, I started looking into what opportunities I had in this new place. Naturally I began with the things I enjoyed and wanted to do and decided to start another motorcycle repair shop. It excited me and I was capable of doing it, but I had left some important shop tools back in PA that I needed in order to open my own shop.

I had to find replacements, which led to me ending up on a tool truck. That's where I met Bruce, the local tool dealer. After my second visit, and a couple of thousand dollars of tools later, Bruce told me that this would be his last year in business and he was retiring after twenty-five years in the tool trade.

"Have you enjoyed it?" I asked.

He replied affirmatively and mentioned that the business had kept his wife and three children fed and housed for over two decades.

This got me thinking. One of the biggest complaints I had about the repair business was the employees - and of course there's always that one customer who wants to cause problems no matter what you do. The fact that you have to rely on a customer showing up for you, compared to the tool truck where you drive to the customer, guarantees that you have a customer. Then, I started thinking about what Bruce was doing. He had a set customer list, or a route, and he was an owner/operator with no employees. The business model was appealing to me because the business had a point of entry that I could afford with franchisor financing.

This was how it all started for me.

I must reiterate that there was nothing special about me. You don't need to be a mechanic or even in that line of work to be a tool truck owner. The adaptation of tools and the mechanical mindset is a plus but not a necessity. Some of the best tool business owners I've seen weren't in that line of work. They're really good at running a business and selling tools, and that makes them very successful franchise owners. During my time as a tool franchise owner in my region, I was in the top 5% with a couple of other guys. This means I was running an average of $950,000 to over $1 million in gross revenue per year. This business made a kid with just a business plan (provided by the franchisor) and $80,000 to his name, to an owner that made well over $150k a year.

It isn't for everyone and it's no shortcut to making a living out of tool sales. It requires a lot of grit, which I consider to be comprised of these important factors:

1. Strong work ethic
2. Time to advance your skills
3. Patience to persevere
4. Determination to do whatever it takes to get it done

Overall in life, grit is hard to find in people and it's even harder to find in a person that actually has the guts to use it!

This is my perspective and the way I made it through all the odds against me. From the professional to personal setbacks to progressive leaps forward, I made and lost a lot of money in this business. This back story is to give you an introduction to who I am and why I'm writing this. I want to give you an overall view of the business so you can decide if it is right for you.

We'll be going through this together, step-by-step, at a high-level of what the business is and what it's really about.

I'll walk you through the operation of the business, how it flows and functions.

I'll explain how to acquire a tool route, beginning with assessing the business with all the options in front of you including the demographics of the area and the drive it involves.

You'll see how to give a valid offer that's understandable to both you and the person that you're dealing with, and we'll look at cash flow so you can see what you should be making for all your efforts and hard work.

I'll explain how to build growth and, finally, after years of success and hopefully money well invested, having a valid exit strategy.

I hope this book helps and inspires you. I also suggest letting your family members read it so they can understand your business.

There's an old saying I'm fond of: "the difference between a master and a beginner is that the master failed more times than the beginner has even tried." Let my failures and lessons take you past my accomplishments.

This book is set up for you to understand and be successful in the industry of mobile tool sales. Together, we'll go over one of the most interesting subjects of my life, the tool business. This book is about whether or not you should invest your time and hard-earned money into this field of work. I've spent the majority of my life working on every mechanical thing I can get my hands on. With that and the ten years as a mobile tool dealer in a major flagship company, I give you my insight into the business. So is the tool business worth it or not?

With a mind-boggling 276 million registered cars in the USA and growing at a rate of 2.7% each year, the industry is increasing. Every type of vehicle needs service in one shape or another to stay on the road. This creates demand for repair facilities and employment for the modern-day mechanic, who needs to be armed with an array of equipment to take care of the modern-day car at hand. From hand tools to diagnostic scanners, they need to be supplied and supported. These are just automobile statistics and don't include commercial trucks, airplanes, marine crafts, motorcycles, and other types of small and large engine machines.

Unfortunately, it's not an easy yes or no question, but one with a very winding path with a lot of pitfalls and misconceptions of the business. In this age of the Internet, everyone has a voice and can ramble on to you about their viewpoint. This doesn't mean they've walked the walk. They'll surely come up in your Internet searches and video thumbnails with a ton of wannabes that never did anything of substance in this business. I'm here to give you my decade-long experience in the business and what it's all about. You'll get a perspective not shared with many people. You'll get to see if this is a viable path for you. I say that because this is a definite option for a life path, but it's an all-encompassing business that can give you the highest highs and lowest lows. We're going to go over how the business operates, how to find a business for sale, how to make an offer on the business, and then how to successfully run a tool truck. I've added many insider tips, which some dealers who are currently in the business need to learn themselves. This includes the discovery of a business for sale to the purchase of the business and then taking you through the metrics of the business, from what it costs to start and maintain it, to the almighty question of "how much will I make?"

Ready? Let's jump in.

Chapter One

What is a Tool Truck About?

AS YOU'VE PICKED UP this book, I assume you're interested in learning about the tool truck business. Congratulations: you're about to learn all about it, including how to get started in it yourself. Before we start, I need to address a common question: "I've seen tool trucks before, but what do they actually *do*?"

Put simply, a tool truck is a truck that sells, repairs, and finances tools. They're similar to a store, except that whereas a store is situated in one place, the trucks run a set route, stopping at allocated points along the way to sell and service tools. Auto mechanics usually make up the base of the customers, but non-traditional skilled laborers also make use of the trucks.

There are two types of business models for tool trucks: independent and franchised. With the franchise model, you're selling tools from that company and you have certain benefits like additional financing options and a network of other franchisees. With the independent model, you're on your own. It's entirely self-financed and you sell tools from wherever you choose. As most of my experience has been in the franchised area, that's where the focus of this book will be.

I have always been told the tool truck business is a cakewalk. You just go around with cool tools and talk to your buddies all day long, cash those huge checks and drive a sweet truck around with no bosses or clock to punch. Sadly, that couldn't be farther from the truth. It's hard work with a ton of sacrifice required to make a valid run at it. But it can also be a very rewarding business, both financially and for the experiences you'll have.

For legal reasons, I won't name the franchise companies by name, and instead will simply refer to them as flagship companies for the rest of the book. As a franchisee, the structure of each business is very similar regardless of which flagship company you choose to work with. The basic operation is to buy, sell, collect, repeat. Of course, each flagship company has its own ways of charging fees, and slight differences in the sales programs, but overall, the structure is very similar. In this book, we'll be looking at the overall franchise model rather than the nuances of each company.

As with any industry, each flagship company has its own reputation and they all claim to be better at something than their competitors (and, in fairness, each is probably better at some things than the others). As an industry practitioner, it's up to you to decide which one you align with, and opinions do vary. I based my opinion on their performance - nothing is more convincing than money, and a company's finances are a good reference point on what and how they're doing. Every flagship company is in partnership with its franchisees, which means that if the company isn't making money, neither are the owners of the routes i.e. *you*.

Before choosing which company, you'll also want to know who owns each one. If the parent company decides to change the direction of the business model, you'll want to know. Equally, if the company is publicly traded then it will answer primarily to shareholders rather than its franchisees; it can still be profitable for you, but knowing who you're doing business with is good due diligence. It's also important to know where their product is produced, since you'll be representing them. Your knowledge of the company's reputation and what its products stand for means more than you know at this point; after all, you'll become their face soon and it'll become a part of your identity. When I started my tool franchise, I lost my identity for the next decade. Rick Murray ceased to exist; instead, I became Mr. Flagship Tool Company.

Each flagship company has its corporate structure. This is broken down into regions controlled by franchise managers, then specific territories controlled by sales managers or developers. Whatever the flagship company refers to them as, they're middle management. This management is your first point of contact with the franchisor. There is also usually a supporting staff to assist in training and sales, and they'll be in contact with you on a daily or weekly basis.

Whichever flagship company you decide to partner with, it's important to know that they have that staff in place. This, to me, is a very valuable part of the franchise model that you are buying into, and one of the clear benefits over the independent model. This is particularly true when you're new to the industry and you've got a lot of customers' needs to fill. That said, not all flagship companies are equal in that respect: some areas are heavily controlled by certain flagship companies, others aren't. But when an area is controlled, a lot of franchise support staff will be in place by the franchisor. This network is a huge help for multiple reasons, one of which is when a customer leaves for another place of employment that may be out of your range, or a neighboring dealer can supply you an item for a customer faster than shipping it. It's also valuable beyond words to have an ally in the field to gauge yourself by and get advice from.

This is a much larger factor than it may first seem. Where else can you go and talk to another local business in the area and not worry about them as competition? Or have a serious talk about the business without the worry of leaking information or letting the competition get one up on you? Being able to do this keeps you informed on what's happening in the area. In this business, it can feel like you're on your own, like a separate island cut off from the world. Having the comradery of a fellow dealer brings it back around for you. I can't count how many times I called a local dealer throughout my career.

One of the franchise limitations is the territory of the route. The flagship company sets the route for your business and you're not able to just go somewhere else if you have a declining area and lack of customers due to that. This is the double-edged sword when talking about territories. Too much territory is great in the sense that you have plenty of customers to sell to, but managing a larger customer base can be extremely difficult and time-consuming, resulting in you spreading yourself too thin and ultimately leading to loss. The franchisor will give you a minimum customer base that you will have as your route. With changing demographics in the area where your route is located, having the franchisor reassess the customer base is very difficult. This fact is proven by the type of area your route is located. If you have a full area with other franchisees, there may not be any open customers for you to take on.

When setting a route, the flagship companies physically go into each shop and ask the employers how many employees they have that purchase their own tools. These people are deemed potential customers, and the number is called a 'customer count'. On an average customer count of 150 customers, a route is made and sold to a franchisee. This is an overall average per industry standards.

The flagship company's brand recognition is also a big factor in the tool industry. The mass amount of cheap tools are always coming from retail box stores and the Internet. They have a terrible brand name, with a reputation for poor-quality tools, known as only being useful for one-time use or the DIY guy. There is no confidence that the cheap company's tools will get the job done day in and day out, let alone be easily replaced if the tool fails. This battle of reputation is played out daily across the Internet.

It's best to stay out of that rabbit hole and understand that all flagships make good products. It really comes down to the tool person, meaning you! Are you going to fix the tool if an issue arises and be able to answer questions both before *and* after the sale of a product? The franchisee that does the most business in an area does so because of his service level, not because his tools are considered superior to the other flagship companies. When you speak to a tool truck customer, they'll tell you who they receive the best service from. The company with the highest praise from the customer will remain supreme in the customer's eyes.

The customers on the routes are a wide range of people and businesses. Traditional auto repair shops, salvage yards, used car lots, large factory dealerships, large truck shops, government complexes, motorcycle repair, boat repair, and some non-traditional stops like a museum that displays restored cars or even a high-end bicycle shop. Not every route in the franchise model is created equal and each route changes drastically within a set area, as you'll see later on.

Your route is the lifeblood of your business. How often you visit each establishment will be determined by the customer's needs and availability; it could be weekly, biweekly, or even just monthly. Each stop is there for you to sell and service the customers. The flagship company will have a pre-setup sales brochure with stock that came in for you to sell. You can also do your own sales program, and this was one of the most enjoyable parts for me. At the stops, you go into the businesses to sell products and collect payments, and you can also take care of any products that need to be repaired or honor warranty from past purchases. If it's a major issue, you have the corporate staff to go to for help. There will be problems that arise, but taking care of the customer is what's most important. As long as you can handle that upfront, behind the scenes you can make as many phone calls to corporate as necessary to resolve a repair or warranty issue.

Your goal on your route is to get as many people as possible to do business with you. Getting customers on the books creates revenue, so you'd better have some people skills. Your customers come in every size, color, and shape, with different backgrounds, religious beliefs, and native languages. They might also not all be who you may expect your typical customers to be. I recall one guy who walked onto the truck in a full karate outfit, looking for a tool to grind a name off a wall in China, where he was traveling to the next day. I found out he owned a dojo next door to a repair shop I was at. Later on, his dojo became a normal weekly stop for me because he wanted tools for his personal use. The lesson I learned that day is everyone can be a customer no matter what, and the business revenue comes from them. How does that revenue come in, you ask? Installment payments!

That might raise some red flags for you, as it did for me when I got into the business. As it's your money you're loaning out by selling those tools on installment payments, it's natural for it to concern you, that's how the business operates. Keep an open mind, though, as we'll get detailed on cash flow and how to be profitable loaning tools on payments later in the book.

The three major parts of the business are the accounts receivable (truck accounts), the inventory, and the actual tool truck. The accounts receivable is financed by you when the tool leaves your possession into the customers. The inventory is bought off the franchisor and controlled by a tool bill. The tool bill is constant in the business since you will always need to be purchasing inventory to sell. The tool bill in layman's terms is like a larger truck account that you keep for your customer. The difference is that purchases will be billed over time frames to the franchisee. We will be explaining the tool bill in depth later on. This gives you the quick overview of the components we will be covering in this book.

So with all of that out of the way, let's start your education of the tool truck business in earnest. To end this opening chapter, I'm including a table of what I think are the top eight pros and cons of the business, and a glossary of key industry terms, which you may want to refer back to as we progress through the book.

Pros and cons of owning a tool truck

Pros

- Cost of entry to franchise ownership can be financed with a percentage of the overall business cost as a down payment
- Make a good living; how much is up to you and your efforts, but the low end is around $60,000 and a higher-end can exceed $200,000.
- Freedom from the normal work-life employer and employee roles.
- The reputation of running your own business and tool provider; the pride of being a tool man.
- Many of the customers and other people you meet in the industry will become lifelong friends.
- Being a tool whore, and experiencing all the newest, best items on the market.
- The franchise model is proven and works.
- It's a challenge.

Cons

- The time involved to make this business work and produce money.
- The incredibly uncomfortable situations loaning money puts you in.
- The stress levels are high.
- Some of the lowest level people you will meet that try or will rip you off.
- Manage a large and expensive inventory.
- The lack of growth, you're set in a specific area and need to purchase more routes to expand the business.
- You have a large loan to pay off.
- It's a challenge.

Glossary

● <u>Account Receivable/Truck Account</u> - These accounts are from purchases made by customers who pay you directly for the product. The business is built on this account. It supplies cash flow for the business, and there is no interest charged.

● <u>Cash flow turn</u> - How many payments it'll take a customer to pay off an account.

● <u>Chargebacks</u> - An amount charged to the franchisee from the flagship credit company. Usually from customers that didn't pay their credit loans or have incorrect contract terms.

● <u>Company credit or Extended Credit</u> - These are accounts owed to the credit company and backed by the flagship company. These have varying Annual Percentage Rates (APR) of interest.

● <u>Collected/collections Sales</u> - A sale that has been paid for, either partially or entirely, in cash or through the flagship credit company. You can see a variety of these terms expressed like "paid sales, completed sales, completed business, etc."

● <u>Credit payment or Credit Collection</u> - The money collected by the franchisee from the customer for their credit account.

- <u>Credit Contracts</u> - A legal contract set up by the franchisee between the customer and the flagship credit company.

- <u>Customer count</u> - The number of people on the route required to purchase tools for their job.

- <u>Discount list price or Tool trade discount allowance (TTA)</u>- The amount of trade or discount you can give on a certain product to still make your profit margins.

- <u>Extended Credit or Credit Sales</u> - Anything sold through the franchisee to the flagship's credit company on a sales contract.

- <u>Flagship Credit Company</u> - A department or company, either backed by or in partnership with the flagship company, to finance the customers' purchases. Very similar to a credit card company, but only securing loans for products the franchisee sells. They set the APR and discounts on various products.

- <u>Promotional Items or Giveaways</u> - Items we give away with a purchase or when a contest is won.

- <u>No Payment/ Customer Skips</u> - Customers that don't pay their bill and vanish, resulting in bad debt.

- <u>Repairs</u> - Items that you repair or send in for repair, depending on the product and purchase date.

- <u>Van/Tool Truck</u> - The vehicle used to drive to customer locations and conduct business on.

-

- <u>Truck account</u> - Revolving account or truck account that gets a payment towards the account, financed by the franchisee from their own funding.

- <u>Purchased Sales</u> - A product that's been sold and delivered to the customer, doesn't show if it was paid for. You can see this in other terms like "delivered sales, open sales, truck payment, timed payment, etc."

- <u>Reason to Buy Now</u> - Used when doing any sales, and giving the customer a reason to buy the product now.

- <u>Warranty</u> - Items that can't be repaired so are traded for new. The cost is covered by the flagship company or manufacture.

Chapter Two

Who Is the Tool Truck Business For?

NOW THAT YOU HAVE A basic overall understanding of what a tool business is, we need to see whether or not it's for you. What kind of lifestyle will you have in this business? How will it impact your personal life with your family? What are some non-negotiable parts of the business - such as the incredibly long days - and what can be changed? We'll be going over all those questions and a lot more in this chapter.

Let's start by understanding that every person and situation is very different. In this book I'm giving you my perspective based on my background and experiences; it won't necessarily be the same for you, but you should be able to apply the information to your own business. Certainly, none of this is legal or financial advice.

Everyone is different: some people may have a strong sales background and adapt to the sales game easily, others may have a mechanics background and have a strong understanding of the industry; some people may have a great ability with numbers and can understand the business aspects quickly, others may have a great customer service background. The list can go on and on. The point is, you - and everyone else - will be stronger in one area and weaker in another area.

The one common denominator for everyone is grit. This is so important that I'll call it the Survival Feature. In the business world, you'll need grit to survive just like water, food, or shelter. In fact, if you don't think you have it, set the book down and go do something else. I don't know if this is a teachable trait since no one taught it to me, but I believe it's something you either have or don't have.

Grit, to me, is innate, but it consists of five essential and learnable skills:

- hard work

- time management

- ability to prioritize

- determination

- and an overall pride and self-accountability for your actions.

Trust me, I was not the smartest, most adaptable or super personable guy in the business, and there wasn't a particular skill I excelled at. All I had was the grit to not give up, ever. If you know yourself and you quit on a lot of things and give in with ease, again, please put this book down and have a wonderful life doing something else, because this business isn't for you.

If you're still reading, that must mean you have some level of grit in you. So let's get to work and dive into the skills. Let me remind you straight away that even the best veterans of this business need constant improvement and are always searching for ways of improving their skills. Try not to be upset if you think you're no good at any or all of the skills, because just knowing you need to improve is a huge victory. Improving on these skills is going to be a lifetime goal. The most successful and influential people that I've had the privilege of knowing all make it a top priority to keep learning, developing, and applying their skills. If you want to climb the success ladder, keep in mind to always pick up a book, go to a class, take a seminar, listen to a podcast, and generally do whatever you can to gain additional knowledge.

Before we continue, I need to talk a little about mindset. The most common mindset is to be a consumer. We all witness it every day, it's the mindset that says "Oh, look at the great deal I got on this product/new car/fancy vacation." We see it in people standing in line for three hours, or endlessly scrolling on their phones for a dopamine hit. There is an abundance of consumerism for instant gratification, but a reluctance to spend money on something that can benefit you over time. In other words, people will spend a lot of money on items that lose value, like cars and clothes, but tell you that investing in yourself or your business is "risky."

I saw examples of this frequently in franchise owners. A deal would come through the flagship company for fifty ratchets at a sale price of $125, reduced from the normal list price of $150. Your first reaction may be to be scared of spending $6,250 to purchase them, because they may not sell. The success mindset says "let's grab these fifty ratchets and think of how to sell them for a profit!" Even if you sell them at the normal list price of $150, you've made an above normal profit of $1,250. If you sell them at their typical retail price on your truck of $150, and with that $1250 dollar above your profit margin. Then use that for a contest prize, say a mini dirt bike, it gives the customer to buy for the chance to win!

The last and most important point I will make about mindset is the ability to loan and collect money. This is a lot harder than you might think. Dealing with this day in and day out can eat you up inside. Not knowing if the customer will pay you at all can cause lost sleep. The flagship company taught me a mindset trick how to handle each and every customer, called the Three F's of Customer Service (confusingly, there are also Three F's of Selling, which we'll get to in later chapters). The three F's are Firm, Friendly, and Fair. This is how your attitude needs to be at all times on the tool truck. Is it easy to be that way? Of course not! It's just a mindset you need to put yourself into doing your best to be there at all times.

With all that said, let's look at the basic skills you should have an understanding of to get into the tool business. We'll start with two that people often mix up: sales and marketing. Both focus on encouraging someone to invest in your product and service, but they do so in entirely different ways. By definition, sales refers to all activities that lead to the *selling* of goods and services. Marketing, on the other hand, is the process of getting people *interested* in your goods and services. With sales skills, you need to be comfortable communicating with everyone and anyone at any time, clearly and confidently explaining the features and benefits of products. Shying away from engaging people is easy to do and needs to be a focus for improvement. Marketing generates interest that can lead to a sale. Remember those fifty ratchets? The contest with the prize is your marketing and a great reason for your customers to buy now. Explaining the features of the ratchet and the benefits of it is your sales. Both are different skills that play off each other.

    There was a quote I always told my customers "I never sold a tool in my life; I'm just a solution provider." This is the mindset you need to have. You're not trying to separate people from their money, you're solving a genuine problem. Customers use their tools all day to perform their jobs, and will eventually run into issues with them. I just showed them the solution and gave them a reason to invest. The linking of sales and marketing relationships benefits everyone involved. You're there to mix the two together so the customer is happy and involved, meaning that they understand the product, while the marketing keeps them coming back to you, which overall keeps you in business. Your interaction with the customer each week will build relationships for more business in the future. Unlike most salespeople, you see your customers each week so get up to fifty-two times a year to sell a product to them. This gives you the time to build trust and respect from them, while also giving you the ability to learn and grow your skills. Don't worry if you don't have a background in sales or marketing; when I started in the business, I had never sold anything formally, it was all motorcycles or repair jobs. You can sharpen this skill on the route with your customers, along with your knowledge of the product. What I mean by this is you can ask the customers questions about the use of a certain tool. The industry you're getting into is all about mechanics. The mechanic loves nothing more than to explain how they fix things, especially what tools they used to do it, so ask them, "Hey, we got this new tool in but I'm not quite sure how it works, let me know your thoughts?" In truth, you may know exactly what it does and how it's better than what they're currently using, but by letting the customer set you straight on this tool, the mechanic tells you all the things they can see about it. With some helping salesmanship, the mechanic can talk himself into buying the product - especially when you give a "special discount" for their help. This is an example of relationship building. Of course, don't do this every single day but it's a good idea to sprinkle it in occasionally (and you may even learn something from it). There will be some time you need to dedicate to learning and mastering some tools, especially diagnostic equipment. Taking a training course and self-learning will help you become more knowledgeable on those types of products.

This book is called *Chasing Twenties* because it feels like that's what you're doing a lot of the time. It's the skill of collections, which is very difficult for most people, including me. Fortunately, I've watched the skilled veterans of this industry do it for years. Now I can help you understand the skill level involved here. Like I said before, this business will push you in many different and sometimes uncomfortable ways. The business forces you to develop this skill. It doesn't get any more awkward than asking for money owed to you, especially from people that'll make you feel like a leper for accepting what was previously agreed upon. I've had this range from easy to nasty; one owner actually locked himself in his office or acted like I wasn't there. When approached, he would get agitated about paying the bill, which required some careful customer service skill to overcome. This is the action of collecting money and it has a very fine line. You have one side where you need to get paid to stay in business, and you have the other side where you want to have repeat customers without making them angry. Trust me when I say they're all watching how you handle yourself in this. Setting a tone is important in your business on how other customers deal with you. If they know you're a pushover then why should they pay you when you have an agreed time to get paid? The other side is that you can be known as the jerk collection man that no one wants to deal with and future sales suffer.

This fine line is why I developed my own system of customer training, which I did to have a better way to approach collections. You must train your customers and yourself each and every time business is transacted. One of two things is true for each new customer: they either have no experience with tool trucks, or they have come from another dealer who had their own payment plan program. So for each new customer I got, I would always go over my expectations, and the conversation usually looked like this:

Me: Hey Mr. Jones, I'm so grateful we will do business together. Have you ever had a tool account?

Customer: Yes/No (my response would be the same however they answer).

Me: Great, let me go over how I do this business on this truck. I do my very best to come with the best deals and services that I can each and every time. I treat all my customers the same, like business partners, and I expect to be treated that way in return. I do my part, and you will have to do your part, which is pretty easy and simple for everyone. Your only job is to pay on time. I can set up any payment that works out for both of us. What kind of program is ideal for you?

The customer then replies with their preferred payment program, and we negotiate - we'll get into the negotiation specifics a little later. For now, let's get back to the conversation:

Me: Great, we can do that for you, Mr. Jones. I'm super glad to have you as a partner, and remember our deal because the most annoying part of my business is asking for money. So I don't make a habit of asking for money, I just ask for tools back.

This is all said with professionalism, respect, and a smile to keep the atmosphere light and to the point. By giving the customer insight into my business and explaining the expectation clearly and directly at the first interaction, it starts the training process that will last the duration of the business. This also builds rapport with good customers and word spreads to the bad customers that they can't get away with missing payments. Collections need to be a priority, not an option. The bills that your business incur don't wait, and neither should your collections. I'm not suggesting you should go around with your 300lb bodyguard breaking legs when the customer comes up short, but be aware that problem collections happen way more than you'd like. It's a daily, if not hourly, occurrence on the tool trucks. This is where the 3 F's come back out: Firm, Friendly, and Fair.

Another key skill is time management. Time is your most precious resource, and the ability to plan, control and prioritize it is a powerful skill you should develop. It's an important but often-overlooked part of the business, and that can be a hard pill to swallow, especially if you have a family that requires a lot of your time. Being able to sacrifice that time for the business and find balance is a very difficult skill. It can be heartbreaking if done wrong. You can get easily wrapped up in the business and neglect the rest of your life. To a point you need to do that; the business is like an infant that you need to pay attention to and feed to keep it alive. It's simply a matter of priorities: if your business is not a priority, your success will be limited.

Day-to-day time management is a bit easier, but not by much. Your route will have a planned stop that you make each week, and an average will have ten to fifteen stops. The exact number will depend on your route and area, and could be significantly higher or lower. For instance, a stop at a large car dealership may have more than forty customers, which may take a few hours of your day. Conversely, you might have five stops with just a few customers, taking only an hour or two hours to complete. When you are driving from stop to stop you can not be selling, if you have a good amount of windshield time between stops that needs to be measured and set up for the most efficient manner.

An innate skill you'll develop over time is knowing when to stay at a stop and keep selling and when to move on to more willing customers. It's crucial to remember that you're the boss on the truck and no one will tell you to hurry up, focus on work and move on. This is a reality check for many people, especially if they've always been managed by bosses. You're also responsible for the customer, who may need careful persuasion to not hang out and escape work for a little while. Curbing that behavior in a professional and friendly manner takes people skills.

The last skill that you'll need is the ability to perform math in your head. Remember in school when they said you should learn math problems because you'll use them later on? Well, you'll need them in this business. So mail your old math teacher a fruit basket for teaching you percentages, addition, and subtraction. Don't worry, it's not as difficult as it may sound. Memorizing is not a big part, but it's just knowing your margins and pricing system. Keeping an overall average margin of 30% on the truck means you can find out the cost pretty easily. For example, if I know there's a 10% discount on a certain product, then I also know my cost for it is 40% off the list price. Let's say a customer comes onto the truck and wants a new set of screwdrivers to replace his old, beat-up set from a different company. Let's say the price for a new set is $140, and you know that you've got a 10% discount, which is $14. The customer's reluctant to pay $140, so you offer to buy his old set.

Amazed, the customer laughs and says "What would you give me, five bucks?"

"I can give you $10 right now, and a new hat since you want to give me a down payment today." (notice how I threw in the down payment as a part of the deal)

The customer is surprised and happy to get anything for his used tools, plus a free hat. But the quick math in this example is the 10% discount of $14 made it possible to spend $10 buying the tools and give a $3 hat because everyone loves a deal. You could have offered a $14 discount, but that's bland and boring. Buying the tools and giving a free hat made the customer happy and feel like he got a great deal, and it was only possible because you already knew the sums in your head.

This skill is used all the time, for most purchases. Knowing your margins and what can and can't be done at a moment's notice keeps you moving forward and profitable in sales.

These skills take energy, a lot of energy. That makes for a long day, every day. You're either an energy person or love coffee. Be aware that this is a high-energy, fast-paced business. No one wants to buy from Mr. Sleepy Sad Pants; they want the same thing you want from them, to be positive, energetic, empathetic, and respectful. The truth is you won't be getting that from them; it's a one-way street and you need to be okay with that. You also need to not let things not affect you, like negativity from customers. You're going to get yelled at by upset people if a tool fails, and you'll want to yell at people that don't pay. The ability to think on the fly is a benefit, such as taking the customers' actions and questions and getting solutions that pay you. Like if you see a customer rummaging through their crowded old toolbox, maybe it's time to talk about the toolbox sales going on. Even when they say how slow their shop is, ask if they have all the preventive maintenance tools on hand to check for a leaky head gasket or check that their brake rotor gauge is in good operating order.

Ultimately this business, like any business, requires a certain mindset to be successful. The time you invest and how you implement that time are both big factors. If you're sure you've got what it takes, let's go see if we can get into a tool truck!

Chapter Three

Is There A Tool Truck For Sale?

TO GET STARTED IN THE franchised tool truck business, you need three things: a tool truck, a franchisor, and a truck route. Routes aren't always available but, luckily, there is always a tool truck for sale for the right price. In general, entry of ownership is not particularly expensive, especially when compared to other services and retail establishments; for example, there is no lease like for a brick and mortar store, nor the long list of fees - from insurances to remodeling - that many other physical businesses have.

As for the routes that become available, each dealer has plans and goals for their business. Some have this as a retirement gig, some are lifetime dealers passed down from their parents, and some have a timeframe to run the business for a specific number of years. The huge variant of life is always there, changing plans for everyone. People leave the industry for a multitude of reasons, but all that matters is that it's not as difficult as you may think to find a route for sale.

One of the best ways to find these franchise owners is to speak to the flagship company you're interested in investing in. Fair warning, though: the information they give you is likely to benefit them and their need to fill a certain area. It may not be the area you desire or it may not be serviced by another dealer for good reason. An alternative is simply to speak to the local dealers by hunting them down on the route or social media.

Before deciding on the truck and route, you need to consider what you want out of the business. High up on your list of priorities should be the quality of life you can afford in an area you're considering. For many people, myself included, working close to home is both helpful and more pleasant. For one thing, not having to sit in traffic for an hour will probably make you a lot happier, and nicer to be around.

For myself, I believe in living ten to fifteen minutes' drive from my route. In the first four years of my route, my journey was forty-five minutes without traffic and over an hour with traffic. Moving closer to the route just made my life simpler, and the fact that you can go home to deal with an issue is a huge bonus. Plus, you can't just simply step off the truck and come back tomorrow; there's a whole shut down procedure, which includes backing up the computer systems and charging internal batteries, and the truck needs to be stored in a secure area to reduce the risk of theft. Having a route that covers some distances are out there, make sure you know the pitfalls of a long-range route and the travel times.

A tool truck isn't something you can walk away from. It doesn't drive fast or handle well in traffic. Let me give you a daily occurrence: when nature calls and you have to use the bathroom. The last thing you want to do is go into your customers' place of business and ask to explode in their bathroom (and trust me, their bathrooms aren't ones you want to use) then proceed to sell tools to them. It's just not professional in my opinion. You're there to do a job and get in and out without causing any issue whatsoever. Being able to stop at home to use the bathroom is a big deal, not to mention if your personal life needs your attention, such as the wife or kids are sick or a water pipe burst. You can stay more profitable when you're on the route not driving to and from your home.

This brings up the question of whether you're willing to move before you get into the business. I know, big changes here; I told you this isn't for the scared or weak-hearted. The fact is that it may be an option for you. If it is, it can add a lot of possibilities for you because now you get to pick where you want to be and who you want to deal with. You get to pick the demographic of the area and customer base you get to do business with.

I chose a heavily populated metro area on the coast of San Diego. There's a lot of diversity in the types of available routes all over the USA, from rural to heavy metro. Each area has its own pros and cons. There are some routes that are in junkyards all day, some that are on a military base all day, some that are in race shops and museums, some that are just the traditional dealerships and small repair shops. We have some areas that are on the USA/Mexico border and have a very different way of doing business than the northern San Diego county guys. Areas where no one - and I mean no one - has a Social Security number, so don't speak fluent English and prefer to do business in Spanish. The point is no route is created equal, regardless of what city or town you choose.

Doing your due diligence allows you to get to know the type of area you're dealing with. You get to see the customer base and even if they're likely to invest in their career. This is done by driving around the area and meeting the people by going on a ride-along with a dealer. Yes, most if not all dealers will be happy to let you ride along to see what they do. It's a hard task to judge from the surface because you may never suspect who your customers will be. The people that'll come up and drop thousands of dollars with you will surprise you. Over the years I've had some of the most interesting customers come into the truck. The industry has a lot of so-called non-traditional customers; people who you don't know normally or call on your daily route.

Since you have the power to decide what route suits you, you can view the type of stops and the kind of business they do. Are they mostly main brand dealerships, restoration shops, general repair, alignment only, auto body shops, junkyards, European only, mining facilities, government facilities, farms, or heavy truck repair? The list can go on and on. When viewing the stops, pay attention to whether they're busy or not, if their equipment is old, and if they have the motivation to be successful. These are some key notes to take when looking into the route and the stops on it. These are the places and people that are going to keep you in business and you don't get to change them once you purchase the business. Some customers leave and some get added, but the overall outlay of the route will remain the same.

Being able to connect with the customer base will keep you in business, and stop you ending up on the street with no customers. It's the difference between the mobile warranty trucks with no profit, and the profitable truck that builds your wealth. If you don't speak Spanish and mostly deal with Spanish speaking customers, you'll be unable to connect with them and their culture.

This is very prevalent when dealing with Middle Eastern cultures. I had the hard-knock experience that no one tells you about before getting into business with that culture. For instance, their bartering system includes "my friend, my friend," then offers an insane low price, which can seem rude to Westerners unfamiliar with it. Consequently, I took my first few interactions with Middle Eastern people very personally and to the heart. I later learned that's just how the deals are done in their culture. You may deal with a huge array of people and your goal is to connect with them and give them the service they require. In return, you get the sales you need to stay in business.

Your route's geographical location helps determine the types of customers you'll have and the type of truck needed. Sometimes when looking into a route, the truck may or may not be included in the sale. Maybe the dealer wants to keep it, maybe you just don't want it - if it's too old, perhaps. Sometimes, financing a new truck is a sensible option. Regardless, you have to make a decision on the truck used on the route. Of paramount importance is the storage of the truck. Having a tool truck at your home has its problems. It means everyone can see it - and some people are bold. I've had people knocking on my door late at night and early in the morning looking to get a tool fixed. The scariest incident was when I was targeted by thieves when I wasn't there. I've had several deliveries stolen from my private driveway and front porch, and my home was burglarized not once but twice. What eventually worked for me was storing my truck at a customer's indoor location, along with the package delivery. It was an additional expense, but much cheaper than getting stolen from or having my home burglarized.

I'll share a little side story about the truck I owned for seven years, which came with the route when I purchased the business. It was a twenty-six-foot 1997 International DT466E cab on chassis with a walk through the main cab to the rear. It was thirteen years old and came with a large folder full of receipts of all the work ever done to it. I marveled at how meticulous everything had been tracked and how well taken care of it was. Of course, the size of the truck scared the hell out of me as I thought about the need to drive this beast through tight beach city streets and alleys. The last owner did it for years so surely I could handle it, right? And I did. Over time, my truck driving skills moved up a level.

Unfortunately, the paperwork folder was hungry, and I mean hungry. Ravenous, even. Within eight months of business, the head gasket blew on the route. My heart dropped to my stomach when I saw the milky oil on the dipstick.

"I've got this. I can repair this. I have a truck full of tools!" I told myself.

Then reality started to creep in and I realized I had no time to fix it, let alone do it in my driveway. But the dilemma is that when the truck wheels don't turn, your business stops. So, I loaded up my personal vehicle with products and a computer and went out to see my customers. They understood the situation and paid their bills, which allowed me to make my own payments even while my truck was out of action.

I had to spend $12,000 that week for a new block, radiator, and injectors, but that folder was satisfied for the time being. That truck would have lasted more than another seven years had it not been for new emission laws for clean diesel that made my truck obsolete in the coming year. The prospect of retrofitting an emission system on a 1997 truck for $15,000 wasn't appealing, especially as every heavy line technician I spoke with explained to me that the kits would cause more downtime and issues with the truck long term. But a comparable new truck ranged from $150,000 to over $200,000.

Don't worry if that's out of your reach financially when you're starting out. The idea is to get a used truck or a smaller truck that fits in your budget. But make sure you plan it carefully, as it needs to hold the inventory and navigate your route. Personally, I can't see anything less than an eighteen-footer being adequate when you pretty much live in the truck full time, and keep in mind the smaller the truck the more difficult it will be to hold the required inventory. The saying is "you can't sell what you don't have." The flagship companies will actually require you to carry a certain amount of inventory. The amount varies between companies but my experience is if you're not carrying at least $130,000 to $150,000, you don't have a healthy truck.

Part of this is appearance. A healthy truck needs to look full and abundant to customers. Put it this way: if you walk into a store and the shelves are empty, would you be more or less likely to purchase anything? The answer is less likely, and the same rings true on a tool truck. It looks weak and unhealthy. No one wants to invest in a business that has signs of failure. The appearance of a well-lit truck full of inventory is the first thing your customer sees, and those customers are looking to invest in tools for their work. The customer will also be making a judgment on whether or not you're in this for the long term, which will impact their decision to work with you or not.

Another consideration when choosing a route is the business ecosystem. Each stop has its own, influencing how it's run, and your goal is to look at the overall work amount throughout the route. Be aware that you'll only be getting a snapshot, and it changes over time. Good shops will become bad shops; the currently vacant stores will become packed full of customers. The large dealerships move in or out, along with their forty customers. It changes from one day to the next.

When you're on a ride-along, pay attention to how the dealer treats everyone. This is the person you're following and overcoming, and it's a lot easier to follow a person that ran a good business with healthy customer relationships. You may see areas you can improve on and that's true, but it will require your customers to be trained for working with you. For example, if the current dealer is lenient on collecting payments, you're going to have a difficult task instilling the new requirements in your customers.

Armed with the knowledge of the demographics of the area, plus the type of truck needed for the business, it's now time to look at the market space you're entering. Is there competition in the area, such as other flagship franchisees? If not, why is that? Is it because there's no business to support a tool franchise? Does the competition have a stronghold on the route and it would take you a long time to break into the area? What's the economic climate of that area?

These are all crucial questions that need to be answered. That said, don't over-analyze it to the point that you don't move ahead with your dreams. Getting yourself in a negative mindset is easy to do when looking at the potential hurdles of starting your own franchise, but the fact is a lot of the "advice" you'll receive is from people that have never done it. So be open to listening, but also be mindful of who you listen to and what their experience is.

Lastly, when it comes to the competition of other tool franchises, I can tell you that there is no loyalty in the tool game. It comes down to who has the best product, service, and price for the customer. That's who wins the sale, period. Running a route in an area where a strong dealer is already present is going to be more difficult than a route with a dealer that doesn't care. The reason the route is strong is that the customer base is strong and they have buying power - that area is making money so, of course, a strong dealer will be there. That isn't to say that there's no room for you to also be there. The standard in the industry is that there's an average of $30,000 of sales on a route each week. If the dealer's doing less than that, there are more sales on the table.

Reaching out to the flagship companies in your area to find local franchises available and talking with local franchisees is the best way to interact with them. Finding the person that's in a transition from this business to other life paths will only be found if you go out and look for it.

Chapter Four

What Is Everyone Looking For In This Deal?

NOW THAT YOU'VE DONE some research on your prospective route, with the location, customer base, and type of market, you can make contact with a dealer who wants to sell. Which means it's time to get down to the deal itself.

To understand this deal, we need to break down exactly what's going on. There are three parties involved in this deal: you, the current franchisee, and the franchisor. In this chapter, we're going to look into all sides of this deal so you can understand what each party wants out of it. By understanding the other parties' intentions, you can craft the deal to benefit you while also satisfying everyone's needs. The deal then becomes obtainable for you.

First, it's important to understand that there are only two ways to leave a franchise route. One is a transfer or sale, which is the most beneficial to everyone involved. This involves the current dealer selling to another person and the business being transferred over. It benefits everyone because of the simple fact it's the most cost-effective way for all parties. The customers get a very short time between owners so suffer less from downtime. This makes it better for a new person to walk into an operating route than to restart an open route that hasn't been serviced for an extended period of time. The franchisor prefers to transfer out because it's expensive to find another dealer compared to having someone already in place ready to go. They also prefer it because their revenue stream is still in operation. It also stops the flagship company from taking control of the route so they can shave off a couple stops to another dealer.

The second way to leave a franchise route is when the current franchisee sells the business back to the franchisor, at a discounted rate. This is not beneficial to either the current franchisee or the franchisor because no one is making money, and it leaves customers without service. The only money is made on the discounted tools the franchisor takes back and that's in the franchisor's pockets.

You need to ask yourself what you're looking for in this business. *What* you want, not *why* you want it. When you know what you want, you'll be in the most educated place to make an appropriate deal, rather than jumping into the deep end and hoping you can tread water well enough to survive. Luckily, you have in your hands the information you need to guide you.

Your due diligence should include the current dealer. Aside from ensuring they have a solid area and active tool truck business, you need to understand more about them. They were once just like you, trying to get into the business. Now they're looking for an exit. In this industry, everyone carries a reputation and it's either professional or unprofessional. You can start to form an idea about him from meetings and from other dealers in the region. This will help you deduce if you're dealing with someone likely to make a fair sale or someone who'll try to squeeze every last dime from you.

You might also have the scary option of an open route that the flagship company is telling you about. An open route means no dealer is working that territory. Every situation is different when it comes to these open routes. Usually, the flagship company is eager to fill any open route with a body to service the customer base. In their haste, they can get over enthused about you, telling you that the fields are green and ready to be harvested with the proper person at the helm. I'm not saying that it has never happened, but in my decade in the business, I never witnessed it. It's not impossible, though, especially with flagship companies that have no presence in an area. Usually, the reason that some flagship companies don't have a presence in an area is that the support system isn't there for their dealer to grow into thriving businesses. The larger, more present flagship companies in that area paint a better picture by speaking to the current franchise owners in the surrounding territories. Where the flagship company or the larger company will tell you about the green grass, the local dealer will usually give you much more truth in the matter. If there are multiple dealers, you can really start to understand why the route is open. If the opportunity was so good and juicy, why wouldn't those dealers scoop it up themselves, get a second member of their staff or involve their family or friends? More realistically, there's likely an issue in that area, like the customer count being too low or the market being too weak to support another dealer.

In most cases, successful owners have legitimate reasons for wanting to exit the business. You just need to know what they want out of the deal and why they're selling. What's their motivation to sell? Naturally, the reasons are going to vary vastly from person to person, so getting to know the seller and understanding their reasoning is only going to help you. Generally speaking, there are two reasons a dealer is selling routes: they're moving on to something else (including retirement), or the business is failing.

If the dealer is ready to exit for their own reason - like retirement, burn out, or moving to a different area - you can find out whether there's a deadline they're working to. If it's a retirement or they're moving to another area, they likely have a fixed date that they need to work towards, which gives you some leverage. It also means that the business is likely to be operational and in good condition, so you can make it work.

On the other hand, it's possible that as they know they're leaving, they let standards slip somewhat. That might have weakened the business, and competition springing up as a result. In my case, I got my route from a twenty-five-year veteran in the business, and I was able to breathe new life into the route. As they say, the low hanging fruit wasn't hard to pick. The customers responded to the new management style I had with their pocketbooks. This is the person you ideally want to find; the person that can show you, without a doubt, they can run the business with profits. If they lived it for more than five years making profits, your likelihood of doing the same jumps by tenfold.

If they're leaving because the business is a sinking ship, then you must figure out the reason why. The two major reasons that routes fail are either the person behind it is messing up, or outside issues are causing it to fail - such as economic challenges or a rezoning of commercial space. Both are fairly easy to determine with some due diligence. We're going to explore due diligence in more detail in the next chapter, but for now, be aware that your offer and ability to purchase the business can change based on why the business is failing. After all, no one wants a route that has a history of failed dealers. Having multiple people go out and try but fail to make the business work should throw some major red flags up in your face. It's not all doom and gloom, though; I've repeatedly seen it where a tool truck isn't profitable simply because the dealer isn't competent, and there's an opportunity to improve matters.

Knowing why the dealer is departing, and coming to terms with it, will make it so that you come out on top. There will be a day when you're exiting the business, also. Your exit strategy should already be laid out before getting into this business, or any business, in fact. My opinion on it is that the exit plan should be the first step in your business plan.

Let me explain. When you get into your franchise, the flagship company will have your business plan laid out for you with a budget. This is the recipe that will get you a franchise. It's the reason you're paying the flagship company money to do business with them. They've been successful in this process and will help you succeed, too. What you need to do is plan for the exit, whenever or however that may be. The flagship won't help you with this, unless it benefits them. So, maybe you will run the business for ten years or even twenty-five years, but you should have your exit strategy lined up from the start, along with the emergency exit strategies because life is fast and hard at times. Having a plan can save you, and not having a plan will cost you.

Another key point in the franchise model is that your franchise is marketable and holds value, which means there's a market to sell it.

Whether it's on a business broker website or Craigslist, it's a marketable asset with value in the brand. The flagship company will have its finger on your business and know whether you are planning an exit or failing out. It'll also have a list of prospects that may have been trying to get into the business. Those candidates are the strongest to get in because they have the requirements to get into the business and the flagship has already vetted them. The requirements are capital and credit scores - they get you to the table. Flagships are in the business of making a profit, and to do that their dealers need to be capable of doing this business financially and professionally. Beyond that, the flagship has the support team to help you carry out the day-to-day operations.

Every flagship company has its own specific requirements for getting into the business, and the easiest way to find out what they are is with an exploratory phone call.

The quick breakdown of a route is three parts: the truck, inventory, and accounts receivable. Overall business costs range from $250,000 to in excess of $400,000, and unless you want to drop that much hard cash, finance it out and play with their money. There's an interest rate, no doubt about it, but that rate is a small barrier to be able to try out a business worth over a quarter of a million dollars. Getting a business loan - through a traditional SBA or bank loans - isn't the simplest task to perform when the flagship company is willing to finance you for it.

Take into account that I'm pretty conservative when investing in any business. To me, having $60,000 in cash reserves to get into the business gives you a somewhat healthy start. My reasoning is that you're going to finance this business. Use my case as an example. In 2010 I paid around $225,000 from a retiring dealer: $120,000 in inventory, $80,000 in accounts receivable, and $25,000 for a 1997 international dt466e truck. I got a $225,000 business for $26,000 down, plus an additional $7,000 in franchisee fees for transferring. I saw that the numbers my route was producing weren't great, but I also saw the potential in the business. The retiring veteran stopped growing the business years ago and just maintained it, and I eventually generated over $200,000 a year of net income. Don't get blinded by that number, though; it took years to build up to that return. My first year in business was rough as hell, but I managed to take home the Rookie of the Year award with over $750,000 in sales. That netted $120,000 in my bank account. All of that business and I was only out of pocket $26,000; the remaining $199,000 was on an interest-bearing loan that I paid off in three years. (You don't have to clear it that quickly; many pay it off over five or ten years, but I prefer to eliminate loans as quickly as possible.)

Now that we've covered how and why to understand the dealer's exit goals, and that flagship company's requirements, we're going to move on to how to do the deal.

Chapter Five

Business Value or Business Worth?

TO WORK OUT WHAT THE business is worth, we need to understand the value of its individual components. There are three major pieces to evaluate: the inventory, truck, and accounts receivable. The value of each of these will differ from business to business - one flagship company toolbox or socket set may be more expensive than another flagship company's - but the core components of how the business operates are the same. We'll go over how to evaluate each part and apply a fair market value.

The first component is the inventory. Sounds simple enough: the goods that are in the dealer's possession and for sale to the customers. Inventory has value just through ownership, but how do we know the value?

In the industry, it's standard to have an average of 25% to 40% mark-up on non-sale items. Therefore, you can usually put an average of 32% to 33% mark-up on traditional stock items in the inventory. Sale items vary depending on what the dealer purchased the item for. For example, if a socket set is a BOGO (buy one and get one free), the sale is roughly a 49% discount. Buy the metric socket set for $200 and get the SAE set for free (value $190). This can add up quickly, particularly if the dealer bought twenty-five sets. Most larger items in the inventory also come in with what's called "trade allowance" or sale price. This is the discount that can be given to the customer if they trade in another item. For example, if a customer wants to upgrade his toolbox to a newer, larger one, they will have an old box that they want to trade-in. The same principle as a car dealership practices; in fact, I have used car dealership slang to sell toolboxes, for example, "push, pull, or drag your toolbox in for a great deal on a new one!" Needless to say, you must understand what the cost differences are in the inventory in order to understand the value of the inventory.

The other thing to look at is the dead inventory. This is inventory that hasn't been sold for a long time. The packaging looks like it's been beaten with a baseball bat, or it's for a car that's no longer popular or even seen in the repair shops anymore. It's usually on a back shelf buried, hoping and praying someone buys it.

Dead inventory can give you more insight into the business the current dealer runs. Is the inventory displayed well, and is there a good amount of selection? There shouldn't be a ton of old inventory sitting on dusty shelves. Most dealers will show you a garage or warehouse full of excess inventory. This inventory is not on display but in a storage place. This is not a sign of a healthy business unless they turnover that warehouse every couple of months. If not, this is dead money sitting on that dealer's dime. This can easily happen to a dealer because of time restraints and overlapping inventory shipments. It is a lot easier to sell an item that you can see and touch. A healthy business knows the limit of excess inventory. A business does need back up inventory, of course, but a healthy limit is around $5,000 of dealer cost. There can be a toolbox in storage waiting to be loaded up, but no more than two.

The excess inventory gives you an idea of what's going on in the business. A healthy business has a good turnover of a product that's well displayed. An unhealthy business may look fine with a big warehouse full of tools, but excess inventory dollars are a sign that something's wrong. Either the dealer's a poor manager of inventory, or, worse, has a bad relationship with the flagship company - this unsold inventory can be the result of not sending it back to the franchisor due to the product being shelf worn or dead inventory.

A lot of, if not all, dead inventory is non-returnable to the flagship company. In fact, it's difficult to return any inventory to the franchisor. This is a fact you need to come to terms with; the franchisor is in the business of selling you tools. I'll repeat this a lot through the book just to make sure you don't forget. The flagship companies will do things like a 365-day lowest price paid return policy. This is where they'll only give credit back to the dealer at the lowest sale price the dealer paid for the tool during a 365-day period from the last purchase price. This means if you got those socket sets for 49% off, sold them, and then ordered another set six months later at full list price, you can't send any of those original sockets back until the 365 days have passed on the 49% deal. If you do return the tool before that, you'll only receive the lowest purchase price in that time period.

The flagship companies don't like returned items; it's bad for their bottom line. Knowing this fact should help you make decisions when purchasing stock from the selling dealer. The types of stock that the current dealer might have other than the flagship company's orders are aftermarket items and promotional items. Both of these are important to have on a tool truck but they need to be priced for what they are, which is a non-returnable item. Just know that if it doesn't sell then it's coming out of your bottom line.

You should know that inventory on the flagship items are roughly 30% marked up, and for the sale items plus a couple of points. Normal stock inventory from the flagship companies has the most value of all the inventory, because it's sellable to the franchisor in a worst-case scenario. For example, in the case of death, divorce, illness or injury and you had to sell everything off as fast as possible for the most value. The aftermarket items and promotional items do hold value, but not as much as the stock inventory from the flagship company. These items are negotiable like all the rest of the business, and working out a deal with the current dealer is best for him. He doesn't want a garage full of inventory after the sale of the business, only to sell the items through online sources where he'll get little value and lose time. That said, it can happen that the current dealer gets caught up in the cost of the value of the promotional items and then calls off the sale of a business. This is usually a relatively low amount of money in respect to the rest of the business, under $10,000 in that inventory. By negotiating properly and with the understanding that the current dealer has a value in his head of what the value of these items are, you can help move the deal along.

The other physical asset of the business is the tool truck itself. There is no Kelley Blue Book pricing to look up a tool truck value. The tool trucks are custom-built vehicles that serve one purpose: to sell tools in a well-lit and organized manner. It isn't feasible for me to list every add-on and accessory associated with each and every tool truck. The core of what you need from your tool truck is knowing if it's reliable, safe to operate, and has adequate space for inventory. The fair market value of the trucks can be easily found online by looking at vendor sites and used tool truck sites. Other great sources are local dealers by talking to them about their trucks and, of course, the one you may be interested in. This also gives you some hints on the reliability of the truck when there are rumors that the dealer always has the truck in the shop or it has been in accidents. Not surprisingly, this might not be the first thing the selling dealer will tell you.

Fair market value might require you to get financing on the tool truck. This is also a big negotiation point when purchasing the business. You'll need to do your research, matching what's for sale with the business against what you see in the market, either used or new, to the purchasing negotiation. You'll need to check the idle hours, whether or not the maintenance schedule was followed, cab batteries/generator life, mileage, paint/exterior decals, and have a diesel mechanic go over the truck. All of those factors play on the tool truck's value depending on the repairs that may need to be done to bring it up to standard.

The current dealer wants to move the truck with the business and so do you because it usually makes the most sense. This can be clearly communicated to the current dealer - that the current vehicle must be brought to a standard level to negotiate the price. The vehicle must be a solid workhorse. Again, let the dealer know that you did your homework on the truck laws and regulations for diesel trucks in your state. For example, you should research the federal or state clean air acts for diesel trucks and upcoming regulations to your tool truck.

This was a hit on my business seven years in, when the California Air Resource Board (CARB) mandated that I retrofit a $15,000 emission system or not use the truck in the state of California (which was difficult, as my route was in San Diego). I realized this was coming by doing the research needed and I planned on a new truck for the business before the regulations took effect. If I hadn't done my homework, it would have been a painfully expensive miscalculation on business expenses. A properly running tool truck, with a well-lit showroom, is your business. Make sure you choose wisely for your route and budget.

The third piece of the business is the accounts receivable, or truck accounts. This is the only part of the business that isn't a physical asset. Tool truck accounts are money owed to the business for purchases by your customers. This is the most common account in the business, making up to 70% of the business accounts, and normally the first account customers get when doing business with you. When customers come on the tool truck and leave with your products, you give them the option to pay it off in terms. The terms you set up as a payment plan for the customer can vary depending on the level of money they owe, with industry-standard being to have the items paid off in six weeks, up to a maximum of ten weeks.

The tools can be expensive, so payment terms make them more affordable for the customer. They also help your business by giving your customers a mandatory reason to return to the store, which may encourage them to purchase more products. This builds the account, creating larger payments that equal larger cash flow.

The number of weeks that it takes for the customer to pay off their products is called the "turn." Reviewing the turn in a business can help you to see the health of the accounts. With larger accounts receivable, the turn can be much higher; industry standard is eight to ten weeks, but with the larger accounts it can go up to possibly twenty weeks. That can still be a healthy business, if the cash flow is the right amount to withstand the purchases, but it can look out of whack due to the payment schedules of the customers. Just as no two stops are alike, there can be significant variances in customers' paychecks. I had customers paying me when they got paid, meaning it could be weekly, biweekly, or even monthly.

When looking into a business account receivable on a tool truck, the average over time is the most accurate way to judge if the business has good or bad accounts. This is done by looking at the collection amounts for the month versus the purchased sales. Is the business selling more than it's collecting on average? These numbers will most likely not be spot on to each other because of the credit sales programs done inside the business to outside credit purchases. These outside credit purchases are paid immediately to the business - we'll go over this in detail later on, but for now, the health of the tool truck accounts is what you need to assess and you do that by looking into the averages. You need to see if there are dead accounts that aren't getting collected from, or accounts that don't have a good turn.

Here's an example of how truck accounts happen and the cost of doing business: Dan is a customer you have done business with in the past, but his account is all paid off. He comes to your tool truck with a zero balance and needs a new cordless impact gun. You sell him an impact gun for $399 plus tax, totaling $430. You and Dan talk about the terms and both agree on a payment plan of $50 a week. He hands you only $40 dollars today, for his down payment. This leaves $390 left on his account with an eight-week turn on the truck account. Remember that the $40 payment just covered the sales tax for the transaction. So next week you show up at the shop and see Dan, and he has some broken tools for a warranty that you take care of and replace for him. You show Dan the newest tool on the market and collect his payment of $50 for the impact gun. On the following week's visit, Dan mentions he's in need of a new ratchet. He has lost his ratchet and gets a new one from you, costing $150 plus tax, totaling $162. This puts Dan's truck account at $502, and Dan explains he can still only afford $50 a week. This will push your turn to the ten weeks max you've set up for a healthy business. So, reluctantly, you agree to keep the payments at $50 a week. Everything is still good in Dan's account. He paid you the $50 payment and his total account is now

$452. Then, two days later, he calls you up and needs an emergency tool to complete a job on a BMW. To fix it he needs a $300 tool, which you can get to Dan very easily. You want to be the hero and get the necessary tools to complete the job, so you run over to the shop. Dan explains he has no money today to pay for it, but as soon as the job is completed, he will pay you more money. He now has a $776 total account, with the tool of $324 (with tax) added to his existing account of $452. This went from an eight-week turn on cash flow to a sixteen-week turn very easily.

    The above example happens every day in the business. These accounts can become dead accounts, if payments stop or lapse over forty-five days of non-collections. I use forty-five days due to the fact some customers pay monthly, although I suggest not to do that in your business because it can throw the averages out of whack and can cause nonpayment on a larger scale if payments are missed. Missed payments are just a part of the business. They're also the hardest part and it's not a case of *if* it will happen, but *when* and for how much. Unfortunately skips, or non-paying customers, do exist and need to be recognized when reviewing the books. You must see the number of skips and their total cost to the business in the past. This will give you an idea of what to expect and what not to include with the sale of the business. Please also remember in the example just given that the sales tax was already added to the accounts receivable and paid by the franchisee. That gets paid first, then the flagship company gets paid for the cost of goods. The bottom line is that skips cost the business the price of the tools *and* the sales tax paid to the state.

    The next thing to know is the credit sales part of the business. This is the most complicated and confusing part of the business, so a lot of people truly don't understand it. Unfortunately for them, it's also a key part of the business needed to be profitable.

    Each flagship has its own programs and liabilities, and it's your duty to know and understand the process when making a decision on the business. We'll get into the more detailed aspects of credit sales and those liabilities later on. For now, the basic point on credit sales is they're the sale of a truck account over to a credit account or a new sale into the flagship credit program.

We can take our previous example of Dan and his truck account balance of $776. He'll need to qualify for the flagship credit program, which is done by running a credit application for the customer, much like applying for a credit card. This is a combination of outside credit history and credit history with the flagship credit company. The credit limit is used to see how much a dealer can sell to him on that line of credit. Let's say Dan qualifies for a $3000 credit limit on the flagship credit account. This means you can sell him up to $3000 worth of products and get paid instantly for it. This is why it's important to understand the credit sales part of the business; it's a piece of the business that becomes very lucrative. These credit accounts are the same as a general credit card from Mastercard or Visa, but instead of being backed by a credit card company or a bank, they're backed by the flagship company, which can be external or internal depending on the company. Flagships have interest rates that vary just like a credit card, in general. All the tool companies' credit programs range between 1% and 30%. This is all dependent on the loan amount and the credit score of the customer.

What you need to know now is how the credit sales work and how it affects the business. For Dan and his $3000 credit limit, you can take that $776 truck account and sell it over to the credit program. This will pay you the $776, but now there is more money for Dan to make additional purchases. What a great time to try to sell more products or a larger one like a toolbox. This is where you do a lot of your upselling for more profits and give the customers the tools they want at a lower payment. This payment can be spread out over five years. Flagship credit makes it easier for the customer to obtain your product even if they are paying interest, just like any other loan.

Finding out the current credit limits for all the customers on a route is important. The current dealer should have been doing his job and keeping records up to date to give you the limits. If this isn't always the case it will result in missed opportunities by the current dealer. It takes time for a dealer to do these credit checks every six months. These credit check programs get the customers to update their information with the credit company, and they can be done more effectively by giving away a promotional item for signing up. Usually, the customers don't want their credit checked unless you give them something for free. But by doing this you can gauge their buying power with you. By seeing the current limits of all customers, and their history of credit sales in the business, you'll get a clearer picture of the health of the business.

Each flagship company has its own credit programs and teams, and a different set of rules and liabilities. Finding out these rules and liabilities is very important. This is going to factor in 30% or more of your business income, so having knowledge of the credit limits and their rules adds value to the business you're interested in buying.

The history and current values on the accounts receivable and the credit sales can and should be easily supplied by the current dealer. Each franchise system will be tracking these numbers very closely with each business. If a current dealer can't or won't provide them to you, walk away. Don't waste your time. You might be wondering why the past has anything to do with the future of the business, that you can't sell the same tools to the same customers again. The reality is that customers will buy several sets over the years. The customers don't only want one set of products like screwdrivers; the products you can provide are practically endless. The new tools that come out from every source are staggering and very hard to keep up with. Worrying about running out of inventory to sell is null and void. Besides, customers lose screwdrivers all the time or they might need replacing. Sometimes the customers love them so much that they buy a set for home or for a gift.

Looking at the sales history tells you not only if the dealer was successful and to what degree, but also gauges the customer base on the route. No one wants a route where the customers aren't investing in tools with you. We're looking for the flow of the business, which might be good or bad. It could be lacking for a multitude of reasons.

The dealer could have struggled in the past due to personal issues like family, health, or a downward spiral of the route's territory. This is mainly discovered with your due diligence and investigation of the business.

There are terms you'll need to get familiar with to understand the history of accounts receivable, and they can vary between flagship companies. "Collected sales" and "purchased sales" might seem confusing because they seem alike, but collected sales are the most important number to look at because they represent the money collected on sold items, either through credit sales or payments collected on customer accounts. This is how much gross profit your business makes. Purchased sales are how many tools you sold, which you may not have been paid for yet. To stay in business, you always want to have equal or higher purchased sales than collected sales, otherwise the accounts will dry up and you won't have anything to collect on.

Now what should you be looking for with collected sales and credit sales ratio? Each flagship is set up on a gross profit number. Meaning, they don't deduct the cost of goods, insurance, loan fees, or any other expense. This is all done by the dealer because everyone's expenses are different. The flagship company knows that a business should be running 30% credit sales and 70% truck accounts. If a dealer is averaging $10,000 in collected sales a week, $3,000 of that should be from credit sales and $7,000 should be from truck accounts. There will be hard expenses out of the $10,000 gross collected sales, as the cost of goods averages 70%, the taxes depending on the area, and then your adjustable expenses like your loan fees, truck fees, rent for storage, mortgage, promotional items, sales aids, living expenses, and the other fees you can add to the business.

For businesses with larger accounts receivable, the ratio seems to change. When I was running my business, I had accounts receivables that ranged from $60,000 to $300,000, and the larger my accounts receivable went, the higher the ratio went. I did more credit sales when I had larger accounts receivables. When it was lower, I had closer to a 70/30 split.

The 70/30 split in the business shows the health of the sales and that you're not relying on credit sales to make money. Credit sales should make up no more than about a third of the sales because the truck accounts are what provide cash flow and keep you in business. Most of the customer base will also prefer truck accounts due to the fact they won't pay interest on the balances owed. Besides, if your business is like mine, the majority of your transactions will be in the $100 to $300 range, so involving the credit company is counterproductive and some customers may not qualify.

Having those numbers supplied for the business is essential and they're very hard to fudge (although not impossible, by adding false customers or adding payments that were never collected). The next part is to verify the accounts and their flow. This due diligence is done by spending as much time on the truck as the current dealer will allow. Join him on his route to observe how business is conducted and to get to personally know him. Finding out his intentions is a key part of this deal. Also, you'll benefit in the long term by going out on your own on the route and speaking with the customers that you'll be servicing to find out their thoughts on the business and their career goals. After all, this business is set up to help the customer do their job better, faster, and easier.

While on the route, you need to observe the shop and how the work flows inside it. Is the shop a sloppy mess or a professional work environment? Are the employees conducting business, and in what manner? Doing this at each stop is too time consuming, but picking out some of the major shops on the route makes it an easier task. Stopping in at lunchtime with some pizzas is always a conversation starter.

Another tip for your due diligence is to talk to the other local tool dealers in the area. You'll be amazed at the resulting conversation if you stop by with a six-pack of beer after their route. This also lays the groundwork for a good relationship between you and the neighboring dealers, which will come in handy when you need a tool or any help with customers down the road in business.

With this knowledge of the business components, you can get a solid grasp of what they're worth. You'll be able to value them for their true value, not what someone told you they're worth. You'll examine the components that may have a potential for good, or be a detriment to the business. You can then look for opportunities and be able to negotiate unfavorable issues in the business during the purchasing process.

Chapter Six

Understanding the Deal

HERE WE ARE, THEN, ready to do a deal. We've assessed the tool business that we want to purchase and done our due diligence on the previous owner, the customers, and the route. Now it's time to start working on the financials.

It's highly recommended to involve a certified public accountant (CPA) to review the loan and purchase types for tax implications. Given the average tool truck business costs between $200,000 and $500,000 with all the components taken into account, it's a big risk to try it by yourself. If you don't have the money to buy the business, you need to secure financing to close this deal.

Each of the three components - the truck, inventory, and accounts receivable - need financing. Of course, they range in price depending on the route you're buying. Each flagship company will have its own requirements, also, along with some different fees associated with the franchise. We're not going to look at each fee and requirement for every flagship; instead, we're going over the core basics of financing the deal through the flagship companies' credit teams. Each fee and requirement are nominal compared to the overall deal that we'll be reviewing. I'll also explain the deal and negotiations with the current dealer.

The most common way to get financed is through the flagship company's credit team. As I've said before, each flagship has its own credit team, and they have the most experience with financing the business. They've been doing it a long time and know what to expect, which is an advantage over traditional business loans providers. The flagship company team will also issue the loan quicker than a traditional lender. It's possible to get a traditional loan or a small business administration loan (SBA), but as they don't have the experience in dealing with the tool truck business, they often won't release the funds in the required time for you to secure the route.

Whether you choose the flagship company or a different loan provider, any lender will look at your financial health. This includes credit score, liquid assets, home equity, outstanding debts, and any income. The flagship companies will do an initial credit check and financial health review as soon as you start talking to them in the very first process of looking at a current franchise. Not everyone's credit scores and financial life are the same, so loan results are obviously going to vary. But for the sake of moving forward, let's say you get qualified.

Once you're approved, you're ready to start selling tools, right? Well, not quite yet. First, let's take a look at what loans you're qualified for and what they mean to you - these loans will dedicate your budget for the next couple of years. The flagship credit teams like to break down the loans into the major categories of the business: inventory, truck, and accounts receivable. The easiest loan to grasp is the truck loan; it's similar to a car loan or lease except it applies to commercial trucks. You can either get a loan or lease the tool truck, depending on age and costs. Figuring out which fits into your budget often comes down to the tax implications, and your CPA will help you decide the best way to proceed.

Your options are to purchase the existing truck from the current dealer, find a truck on the used market, or buy new. They normally range from $50,000 for a lower-end used truck, to over $200,000 for a newer higher-end truck. There will be trucks available for less than $50,000, but you need something that's in service, dependable, and well maintained. I started out in a $25,000 truck but it cost me a new engine and repairs of $12,000 in 2010 pricing.

Overall, for a tool truck that's ready for business, meaning the inside and outside are clean and ready, you need to be prepared to spend around $100,000 - $120,000 for new startups. These loans are fairly easy to grasp because it's just an auto loan with commercial loan pricing. If they're so easy, why do I recommend hiring a CPA? Because the trucks are a depreciating asset and the loans are tax write-offs.

The accounts receivable loan for each flagship company will also differ, so I'll go over what I'm used to seeing in these loans. They'll normally loan up to 75% of the accounts receivable. Let's recall the cost of goods (COG) is 70%, so they normally don't finance the dealer's profits. So, let's use an example of a dealer having an account receivable of $100,000, making $70,000 financeable. By your due diligence and review of the accounts receivable in the last chapter, you should know if the accounts are in good standing.

The next part to get financed is the inventory, which again varies from lender to lender. My experience is that they'll finance 75% of the list price of the products in the inventory. Let's say the current dealer has $150,000 in inventory. The total financed amount is a $112,500 loan. This is on qualified products in the inventory, meaning discontinued or worn products don't count. Also, promotional items like hats, shirts, and other giveaways won't be financed. Knowing this, be prepared to negotiate out-of-pocket expenses for those items with the current franchisee.

The other loan that you'll have, and which will never go away, is the tool bill. This is a non-interest-bearing loan for products that you purchase for the business to sell to customers. However, this loan doesn't take effect until you are in business and selling products. It's the biggest expense in the business as it covers the supply of tools you're selling from the truck. This loan must be closely managed by you, otherwise it can get out of control. Left unattended, it can weaken or even sink a business. Each flagship company will set limits on your line of credit; mine was $60,000, but I never went near that limit. There's a risk that you won't sell all that inventory, and it's an unnecessary stress of excess inventory. The tool bill estimation amount is a needed number to help find out your break-even numbers for your budget.

In total, you might have a truck loan of $120,000, inventory of $75,000, and accounts receivable of $112,500, totaling $307,500. The flagship company will want a down payment of around 10%, meaning you can run a $300,000 business for only $30,000. (This was the biggest thing that lured me into the business; everything you buy has value, so if you fail for whatever reason, you're not out every penny.)

This is all financed at the interest rate, which in my case was 9.6%. So now we'll look into the budget, to help eradicate that interest rate. Your budget should incorporate your business and personal life. To do that, you need to find out all the expenses you have, from your wife's shopping sprees to kids' braces to magazine subscriptions; everything in your personal life needs to be accounted for. Being honest and heavy on the personal budget is necessary. The grocery bill might be $120 a week for the family but estimate it at $150 in case the doctor says a new diet calls for special food. Being able to budget for the personal unseen, like the medical emergencies or a car accident, is easily done by setting aside extra for those unexpected expenses. Budget spreadsheets are available everywhere on the Internet and the flagship company will make it mandatory that you fill one out. You need to know what all the expenses are in order to be successful. Taking your partner's income into consideration is needed to help offset some of those expenses. It's somewhat easier with a partner's income so that everything doesn't rely on you. For me, it was the motivation that I needed to bust my back to be successful because I only budgeted for myself. Having that budget dictated what my collected sales had to be. This was my break-even number that had to be hit each week to stay in business.

In addition to your personal numbers, you'll have your business budget with your expenses all listed out. The flagship company will have this locked down to a very close number for what it'll cost you to run this business. They've been doing this a lot longer than you or me and know what to expect for the day-to-day expenses like fuel costs, insurance, storage fees, promotional items, and tool bills. The big ones are the loan payments on the business. The flagship company wants to be paid back and you want to pay them back even faster.

Remember you're running the business on their interest rate. Let's use me at the 9.6% points on that $307,500 loan. That is almost $27,000 a year out of my bottom line to pay just the interest. This is why it's important to understand the loan and see the benefits of it, but also see how important it is to get out from underneath it. The flagship credit company may put you in a five- or ten-year loan on this business. This was fine to me as long as I knew the prepayment penalty, if any, or any other fees associated and disclosed with the loan. The reason it was fine with me was that I wanted out of it as soon as physically possible. That's your money and the pressure to perform well translates into the business.

By now you should have your budget for all expenses totaled up, for personal and business. The total is your break-even number, which is what you need to hit in collected sales each week to break even and stay in business. How will you get to those collected sales? Remember you have the past dealer's numbers, which gives you a solid history of what the business was doing. You need to take into consideration that you're new and may not hit those numbers right off the bat. It's going to take some time to build relationships and learn the route. With that average on what the previous dealer was doing and your learning curve, you can see if the numbers will work out in your favor or not.

When looking at the business through a spreadsheet, you must recall what you can change. For better service and more market share, your hard work and patience will see the business grow - as long as you have the right sales and strategy laid out. But keeping a reserve fund is an insurance policy in case the plan doesn't go as anticipated. The 2020 COVID-19 outbreak, the broken leg or limb, the divorce, the auto accident, the health issue that came up. This is totally up to you to have or not to have. I'm telling you to have it to help ensure your success. This money should be able to hold you and your business afloat for four to six months. The belief in Murphy's law is not a negative view on life, but a smarter way to plan. The worst case is when a dealer gets over-leveraged, then doesn't perform as well as they budgeted for in the collected sales. The expenses outweigh the sales and the dealer still pulls his paycheck. This is where it starts to catch up to the dealer over time. They still have tools on the truck to sell and still have to collect money. Then in that case, the orders for tools, either warranty or sales, don't get filled. The tools on the truck start to look slim because they aren't allowed to order from the flagship company because they're over their tool bill limit. You can live some time off that $120,000 of inventory and initial investment. If you're not refilling the orders because you needed extra money for whatever Murphy's law expense, it only hurts the business.

I also want to make you aware of the unwritten three-year rule. You can live up to three years on the inventory and accounts receivable of your business. After three years you either get it or get out. It also might be the daunting loans that crush the new business owner's spirit. Whatever the reason, the dealers that make it past the three-year mark usually stick around for the long term. This isn't an exact science, but something I observed and have had corroborated by other dealers.

Your budget and required sales goals should be treated as life or death numbers. Hopefully, with some time and the right strategies taken away with this book, you'll be doing more than just breaking even. We didn't get into this just to break even. We're here to make a good living and a better life. With this plan and budget set, we're ready to make an offer on the business, knowing the components of their values and the loan structure means making a strong offer visible to the dealer.

Having this offer written out on paper with the current dealer opens communication on what you're expecting out of the business. Your written plan should show your side of the equation to be successful and where the numbers need to be to obtain that. Most times this is enough to help close the deal with the current dealer, especially if they're motivated to move on. Other times, it's a harsh reality to the dealer to see that their business is not worth as much as they thought. By showing the dealer that you're the means to the end for them financially, physically, and mentally, they can start to see the truth in their business. The tool truck business is not a joke, it's hard on everyone in it. The daily grind wears on the toughest people. On the plus side, it also gives some of the best rewards. The fact that you came this far to make an offer on the business means the dealer has some serious interest in selling.

Keeping a cool head and an open mind will pay off for you in the end. Your ability to tell your story and state your goals to the dealer shows your financial entrance point. That point has to come close to or match the value of the business. If it doesn't, or the dealer wants more than the value, the negotiations start. You have to know what you're willing to invest in this business and then be careful to not go over that number. The difference in the value of the sale can be negotiated in a way that it's payable back over time just like the loans you're already taking out. If the business is any good, then the dealer shouldn't have too many issues with financing the difference over time. This will also show you if the dealer thinks the business will succeed or fail after him. Side deals of any kind with the dealer are common and normally accepted by the dealer. I've seen deals range from guys trading cars to weekly payments, and everything in between. The point is you must be open-minded about closing the deal so everyone feels happy about it.

By doing your homework, you should be able to put together an offering that you consider fair market value for the three major components of the business that you've learned in the previous chapters. Now you should be ready to show the flagship company and the current dealer what you have to offer to make this business thrive and get your return on investment. Simply taking the average collected sales, getting your net income over the year, minus a living salary, and paying extra off on those loans should give you a good idea of what's needed to be successful in that route.

Congratulations, now the work starts.

Chapter Seven

Relationships

RELATIONSHIPS ARE SO important that we're going to spend an entire chapter talking about them. Before I got started in this business, I really thought that I was good at making relationships with people. I was always the type of person where you either loved me or you didn't, and I really didn't care either way.

I needed to change that thought process, and so will you. You're going to have over three hundred people who you *must* have at least a civil relationship with. These people may be directly buying from you or just interacting with your business. The latter group will include your customers' wives, the office personnel that you pull up in front of each week, and any people you interact with. All of them are important if you like staying in business. This is the tool sales and customer service business, which means you better have good to great interpersonal skills with your customers, the flagship company, and everyone in between. These relationships will stretch over and beyond the life of the business.

Every dealer goes through training from the flagship company. The good news is, the training is effective. It stuck with me throughout my career and it's proven itself true and an overall guide on how to act. I learned, and still use, the three F's: Firm, Friendly, and Fair. This is the most effective way to deal with people inside and outside your business. Always keep those three F's in your head when dealing with anyone, and I mean anyone, around you and the business. This includes your vendors, flagship representatives, support staff, customers, and anyone else that may interact with you. This lays the groundwork on how you are as a person and lets everyone know your reactions will be close to the same each and every time they interact with you.

I drive this point home hard because the business and running the route can feel like living on an island. You'll get used to dealing with the customers and the people around the business, like the flagship's reps and other support staff, so keeping a good relationship with everyone on your island is important. Your customers are going to be in contact with you more than the others. Keeping the three F's a standard with them is the best groundwork. It's also the groundwork with everything else. The flagship reps are people, too. It's easy to forget that on your island. They're there to support you and the relationship can be one-sided in either direction.

As a business owner, your goal is to keep the relationship good by doing your part. This means participating in sales meetings, events, and training courses. Sounds simple, right? It is, but all of these things take time, and for everyone in business - including you and me - time is the most precious thing in the world. Time out of the route is time you aren't performing and producing collected sales! Budgeting your time is a hard skill to get right, but it's an essential one. Knowing you need to budget time for flagship company events will ultimately help you professionally and show the flagship company you care about it. You prove to the company that you cared enough to get out of your island to participate in learning new products and sales programs, or to just listen to the direction of the flagship company. Also, you'll be able to see fellow franchisees and get their feedback on what's going on in their business. This is invaluable; after all, they're running a very similar business to yours and what's happening to them most likely will be happening to you also.

Don't get me wrong, the flagship company runs these events to sell you on more products. Their goal is to sell tools and you're their customer. Your goal is to get those tools to the end-user. Not every item, event, or program that the flagship companies come up with is a home run, and it's your job to know what they have in mind and consider how it can work inside your business. The new items that you bring on the truck might be huge money makers and sell out quickly. A good relationship with the flagship reps and having them understand your budget for new products is essential. New products are great, but you don't want to lock up your money in slow movers and the reps can help you disperse excess inventory when needed if they understand your situation.

The million dollar question is how do you tell what's going to be a big mover and what'll be the product that goes over like a fart in church? The unfortunate but honest answer is you don't. There's simply no way to know or predict it. Over the years I've gotten products that I thought would never sell and they were huge moneymakers. I also got products I thought no one could live without and instead no one bought them. But since we kept that relationship strong with the flagship company, they're more willing to help move the product, either to other franchisees or as a return. This is a long-term relationship and keeping it positive is only going to help you. The flagship companies touch on every part of the business. There are going to be problems, which we're going to explore in great detail soon. But trust me, I hurt only myself when I pursued a fight with the flagship company, or anyone in the business for that matter. The reality of this business is you're the end of the line, so the troubles, losses and overall nasties roll on you.

Each major flagship company has systems in place to help the business operate. These systems are wonderful for knowing how to run certain functions, like doing your warranties, back-ordering products, or having a pre-list for customers ready. During the training, the flagship will go over each subject in great detail. After the training program, they have a flagship rep accompany you on the route for a minimum of a month to help you navigate the route and learn the stops. They even train you on factors like traffic drive times to keep the most efficient pace through the route, so you see everyone on a daily schedule that you hadn't even thought of yet. This also helps plan your movements between the stops to get to the timed stops, which are places that only let you in at certain times of the day. This isn't uncommon in large dealerships or manufacturing plants. You'll also have owners of businesses that only want you there at certain times. Dealing with timed stops can be difficult, but it's a part of the business. Things like parking the truck at stops can cause conflicts with the business, along with their hours of operations. Getting to communicate with the customers, from the lowest guy to the owner, is a key part of the relationship. Finding their needs and being able to accommodate them will make you an ally instead of a nuisance. Knowing when most of the employees will be there to conduct business and which days are better for their schedule will also impact your sales and collection numbers. All of these factors need to be worked out with communication and good relationships with the customers. Changes are inevitable and you need to be able to adapt to stay productive and profitable. The help of the franchisee trainer, and your good people skills, will help schedule the route appropriately. It's easy to get caught up in the hurry to the next stop, so it's important to remember that the most important customer is the one standing in front of you. Besides, the fuel and time were already spent to get to that customer, so it's best to make something out of it. I found the flagship training very helpful on these fronts, but what it can't teach you is how to react to customer relations issues.

How you deal with issues with people is totally up to you. The flagship company training can *tell* you how to react to conflicts and objections, but your reactions are up to you. I personally wasn't good at being Mr. Nice Guy with conflicts. This was something that I had to teach myself, with the help of my own customer training program. I used this training program to train my customers and myself, day in and day out, never stopping. It didn't turn me into Mr. Nice Guy, but it did present the conflicts and issues in a set form manner. I learned to structure how I dealt with each person and react the same every time, from a corporate person to a customer and all the people in between.

We do this training with our core three F's always in mind. No matter how much the person is screaming about an issue, remember Firm, Friendly, and Fair attitude. Each person just needs to be educated on what you expect and how the business works. This also goes for you and me, too. I repeated myself over a million times in the ten years, not only for the customer but for me, too, to know the truths of the business and what's needed for its survival. This is the key to unlocking your tool truck business for a much higher rate of success over time.

What do I mean by this? Very simply, at a normal stop when you pull up, do you just hope and pray that someone comes and pays for the tools, hoping that they will sell themselves? If so, then you're setting the customer and yourself up for failure. This concept is not difficult to understand, but I have seen it not executed throughout the business. It's entirely up to you as an owner to have a training program set up. I say program because the plan, desire, or will seems to be time restrictive, but the program is forever and permanent. By training the customers and yourself on a program, the rate of success jumps significantly. Failure has a hard time rearing its ugly head. The training program you run explains to everyone what to expect from the business and how you react to issues. The program will be hard to follow at first but will become easier over time. Eventually, the customers will be more trained on what they expect from you and what you expect from them. This includes being there each week, on time, and providing the best customer service, walking into the shop each week with promo items or the newest tools on the market. This means going in smiling with a firm, friendly, and fair personality because no one wants to deal with a negative person. Even if you get that attitude from people, your talent and professionalism in the program won't allow you to respond in that manner. You must take care of any warranty or broken tool issue quickly and easily, training them and yourself on how to be treated in that same scenario. This is a key aspect of building rapport with the customer by showing them what you can deliver. You're showing them how much they're a part of the business and you're the owner. This is key in giving anyone you do business with the reason to buy and pay in a timely manner.

I've always done this with respect and demanded the same in return. This can be verbally, by talking to the customer outright about how you conduct your business and what's accepted on both sides. You lay the groundwork for your professional relationship in the first meeting, however this is only successful when you stick with the program each day, each week, each quarter - all the time. It's critical for you and the customer to know this is how it is. The secret sauce to the whole interaction is your personality, not a fake persona but who you truly are. No one believes a fake person and you can spot them a mile away. This has to be you inside and out, running a program with a positive and humble personality.

Now, how to grow and gain more of these relationships with the customers? Simply put, this comes with time and effort. There are different ways that this can be accomplished once the customer respects the business and you respect them. Now the way to connect with a customer can be done in many ways. One traditional method is treating good customers to lunches and dinners. It's a great way of just trying to get to know each other better and bonding over a meal. Pushing sales is not the goal of the meal; in fact, that'll only detract from it. The goal is to become more than a customer, so they don't see you as an evil salesman. If time is the issue then stop in with some beers after the workday. I spent many nights chatting about life with owners and employees, becoming more than a salesman to them. These are things that you don't do in the day-to-day operation, but the extra effort grows relationships. This will eventually evolve in doing other activities with customers and flagship reps. I also tried to include people in activities I did for enjoyment if I thought they'd be interested. For example, I undertook my first triathlon with a customer. I also invited them to camping trips and beach parties. It makes you grow as a team with the customer, and now they see you as a person instead of Mr. Tool Company.

This trains the customer that your success is directly related to their success in the field. Driving this further is your ability to hold seminars for the customers. These seminars can be about the variety of products that you provide to them, from diagnostics to welding. Hosting them does come with some expense to your business, but you should reap the rewards. First, you need a venue - a hotel conference room, or your customer's shop if they're willing to provide the space. Then, hire a qualified trainer on the subject manner that you want to sell. The customer will be sitting through a two- or three-hour seminar about your product. The best way to offer the seminar to the customer is not for free but, instead, charging for it. Paid seminars have a 90% attendance rate, but free seminars have just a 50% attendance rate. The customers will be used to paying for training in their field of work. Your goal isn't to make money on the fee for the class, but to get them there to see the sales promotion that's presented during the seminar. Educating the customers on the product and troubleshooting issues in the field is why they're there. You need to deliver that through the trainer and have the solutions for their issues with your product.

I would be remiss if I didn't also include in this chapter a warning of the negatives that will undoubtedly fall into your lap. I do believe I've been blessed with some great relationships and forsaken by some horror stories. The horror stories I'll go over are extreme and you may never have to deal with the same level or degree that I did. And remember: these happened to me over the course of a decade, so they're rare.

With that being said, there are some really bad people in the world and you're likely to meet some of them in this line of work. These people may try to harm you and the business, intentionally or otherwise. They do it in a way that can change your attitude or personality. Even if you do your best and have some superpowers that block negative emotions, it'll find its way into you. Even if you have great armor, it will find the crack in it. The fact is, people are going to steal from you. This isn't a case of "maybe" but "how often."

The likelihood of someone shoplifting from you is very slim, but it's not unheard of. I caught only a very small amount of people shoplifting and most of the time I'd approach them in their shop and ask "can I add that to your account?" They'd usually just say "I thought you already did."

Having three cameras on the truck facing the customer was a strong deterrent. The major issue of theft is the people that skip out on their agreed payment plan. When the customer doesn't pay, it comes directly out of your bottom line. You're essentially paying for their tools and the service you provided to them.

Customers steal by missing their payments and/or disappearing. The measures that some customers go to skip out on you is quite amazing at times. I've had customers move jobs, cities, and even the country, since I'm so close to Mexico. This happens more than you think. They'll block calls, social media, and everything they can just to not hear from you. Sometimes, since the world is pretty small when dealing with a major flagship company, another dealer will find him on their route. The missing customer always has an excuse and no matter what garbage it is, you have to keep your cool and deal with it with your program of firm, friendly, and fair. That will be the only way to get results from them. Threats, yelling, or physical harm will only make things much worse. My predecessor advised me to write down each excuse you hear so that later you could have a great coffee table book called "A Million Excuses Why Not To Pay Your Bills."

Keeping cool is something I had to learn fast. The way I kept focused on being professional was knowing the facts. The fact is, the customer knows they're obligated to pay for their items. That doesn't mean they *will* pay you; in fact, the laws are set up against you. To go the way of the law and pursue the collections in court will cost you more than the customer owes you. The time alone is enough to know that this isn't a viable option. Getting back products or a repo will help minimally with the cost of lost business. Unfortunately, you can't take back time or make the product new again. These are things to take into account when doing business with people you may not completely trust. If you're at the point with a non-paying customer where you have a ton of time sunk into them and have made multiple attempts to get them back on track, you may be at the point of asking for the product back. Again, this needs to be done with the three F's program. This is the hardest time for me to be friendly and fair, when the customer has stolen. By explaining the business to them from the start they should be able to wrap their head around the fact that they're stealing at least "time" from you. This should be the training that you give the customer in this situation, making it clear that it's not okay to not pay, and this is done in a variety of ways. I've had signs on the truck stating it, printed late invoices on red paper, and had the discussion, again, about how the business works. This is all training for them and you.

A common excuse heard on every tool truck is "I'm broke this week. Can I just pay you double next week?" This sounds harmless enough, right? The truth is, they're not going to pay you double next week; in fact, chances are they'll short you next week also. If you let that slide then they know your bill isn't that important. Instead, training them in the right fashion to understand that your bill is very important, and doing so in a manner that's positive and not overly aggressive, makes it stick better.

The rebuttal to the statement "Can I just pay you double next week?" is "No, Mr. Jones, I'm sorry; I can't do that." There is usually silence with a stare. They'll either pay in full or you may get the comment "I just don't have any money."

In that case, respond: "I understand, Mr. Jones, that you're broke and you understand how my business works, so how about you do at least half the payment today?" This emphasizes the urgency of the payment and gives them a solution to the problem.

Let's say in this example the payment is $50; if the customer can do $25, or even $20, it's a positive collection, instead of you using your assets to drive there and not collect any of the payment owed. You can ask if they can borrow the money from someone at the shop to complete the rest. This almost always comes back with a very negative response and a firm "no". My normal response was, "That doesn't seem fair, I loaned you the tools for my paycheck." I would do this in a nonchalant manner, making the customer see what he's asking of me to do.

After letting that settle in the customer's mind I come up with a solution. By doing this I want to come off as a friend. "I really don't want to burden you with a $100 payment next week if you're so broke this week," pausing then looking at them. "How about instead I just change the payment to $60 a week for the next five weeks to make up for the missed payment?"

Normally at this point, the customer is uncomfortable and just wants you out of his face. They usually agree to those terms, but you need to confirm them by making them repeat the payment three times in conversation. For whatever reason, it seems to be the minimum number of times to make it stick in the customer's mind. This is done any way that you can, for example by saying, "Okay, so we're good for how much next week?"

"You're totally comfortable paying how much next week?"

"We're 100% on the payment of…?" or any other way you can come up with to make the customer repeat the new terms.

This is an important part of the business, to make sure you have the cash flow to keep operating. Letting payments slip here and there adds up very quickly. You'll hear some very convincing and compelling excuses, too, ranging from the ridiculous to the heart-breaking. Nonetheless, the fact that a bill is a bill and needs to get paid must be ingrained in every customer's frontal cortex. I learned to view excuses as "at least they're talking to me, though." Silence is the worst when trying to collect money. It's the sound of your money disappearing.

There is the option of hiring a collection agency, although my experience with them is they have ultra-poor success rates. Each collection agency promised results, and even money-back guarantees, but it was all bogus. The time invested in getting them the information needed to start the collection process versus their results was never worth it. There's also the emotional aspect, as it would put me in a terrible mood when reviewing the people that ripped me off. That mindset is hardly going to put you in the Salesman of the Year category, which is the mood you need to be on 24/7 on the truck.

This leads me to a person who specialized in tool truck collections. I met him online and was warned that his tactics are a lot harsher than the normal collection agency. In this business, you can have a 5% to 10% loss average on collected sales, which is a lot of lost money. So, I figured why not try this last guy out? He worked on a

55/45 split, taking 45% of whatever was collected and giving you 55%. This was somewhat normal in collection companies and 55% is a lot better than 0%. Since the flagship companies don't get involved in the truck accounts collections or repos, we're 100% responsible.

This person did get results at the beginning for me. However, the issues he ended up causing me legally and financially cost me twice what he collected. That isn't even including all the time spent dealing with the messes he caused; unbeknownst to me, he was making threats of calling the police, writing letters to customers and all of their family, and calling their employer constantly. He was an overall nasty guy. The letters and how he represented himself were done under the name of myself and the flagship company, which cost me legal fees and a ton of issues with the flagship company.

There was one particular collection he performed on a customer that I still saw on my route, but who refused to speak to me. It started like all other business starts. I knew and had done business with the customer before. In fact, he was employed at a major dealership for years before I even started in the business, so he had a long history of being an overall good customer, and he was an ASE-certified master mechanic with a large toolbox and tools. One day he said he needed some tools along with a new scanner, which I was delighted to sell to him. The total was in excess of $10,000. Using the flagship credit program to make this purchase, we started our payment plan. The next week rolled around and he needed $500 worth of odds and ends he forgot about in the larger purchase the prior week, which I added to the truck account, collecting payments on both accounts. A couple of weeks pass by as business as usual with the customer, and then I get a call from the flagship credit team. They tell me that the customer has filed for bankruptcy and that I can't ask for any payments on the credit account - I'm allowed to collect, but I can't request the payment. The rules with the credit team are that if an account goes bad then they charge you back 25% of the loan. So naturally, when I saw the customer, I approached him about it. He replied that he wouldn't speak to me and that I had to call his lawyer. This is actually surprisingly common in this line of work, where you can get shafted by different sources you would never think would do that to you.

So here was now a chargeback of $2,500 plus the $500 on the truck account that I wasn't going to get paid on. I sent that over to the collection person and he got the customer to pay back the $500 on the truck account, but not the chargeback money and he also refused to return the tools. In the following weeks, I got another phone call, this time from the flagship company lawyers. This is a first for me. They instructed me that the media would be calling me or paying me a visit that day and to say nothing but "no comment". The flagship lawyers also said that the company wouldn't give any legal advice or help. Now the hairs on the back of my neck are standing up. They started asking for my collection guy's name and phone number. I gave it to them. The lawyers explained to me that my customer was involved in a shooting with seven people, killing one and injuring five more. The customer was killed by the police. Floored by this news, they added that the lawyer representing the customer for the bankruptcy case contacted the flagship company and wanted an undisclosed amount to keep quiet about the collection letters. The angle the lawyer wanted to play was that the letter caused him distress to commit those awful crimes. Later, I found out that the customer had just recently broken up with his girlfriend and was using drugs heavily. He was in financial ruin, owing more than $100,000 in debt from taxes to jewelry. He walked into his apartment complex community pool area where a birthday party was taking place and opened fire on them, eventually getting killed in the crossfire with police. This is an extreme case, and I'm using it to illustrate that sometimes relationships turn bad.

Having this insight about relationships before I went into the tool business would have fast-forwarded my years. Hopefully, this gives you the tools and knowledge to get ahead of the learning curve.

Chapter Eight

Business Flow

IN THIS CHAPTER WE'RE going to cover the basic flow of the business, how we use different metrics of Buy, Sell, Collect, and Repeat to look inside the tool truck business, and provide some insight on the daily, weekly and quarterly operations of the business. This includes the financials for each account and how one feeds another, how the truck accounts build credit sales, and the operations of sales and repairs.

With that, I must stress the energy levels involved to keep a successful tool truck running. The day is long and the daily tasks, from the first stop to the late-night stock orders, take an incredible amount of mental and physical energy. I look at energy as another skill that you need to have in your arsenal; one that you can improve upon with effort and techniques. Some days will be better than others, of course, it just needs to be on the front of your mind at each stop. The fact is that you're the sales force and no one wants to deal with a lazy bump on the log personality.

Having your mind on other facets of the business instead of on the customer is common and also makes it easy to make mistakes. The ability to keep your energy levels up will push your business to that next level, and this is managed by knowing the innumerous energy sucks that get thrown at you throughout the day. They can come in any form that distracts from you performing your task of selling tools and collecting money - customers, the flagship company, the traffic jam, stress at home. They're everywhere and you need to swiftly learn how to deal with them.

By quickly identifying what's in front of you and deciding how to handle it means you can return to your tasks with minimal disruption. Always remember that if you're not selling or collecting, you're wasting time and money. Doing this with a positive mindset is a tremendous task to keep up all day, every day. The level of negativity you get from sales and loaning money is a generator of negative mojo; you need to accept it and deal with it, in the same manner, all the time. It's a major part of your training program for you and the customers.

Negative customers will wipe you out *if* not dealt with in the right manner. It's common for the customer to come onto the truck and complain about anything and everything; you're the vent for a lot of guys that have stressful jobs, and every situation is different. Depending on the person and the heat of their complaints, I'd deal with it in one of two ways. If they're worked up about anything that's causing the complaints and negative attitude, simply let them tire themselves out with the head nod and the occasional "yeah." When that's all done you say "okay then, what can we get today?" If a broken tool is the issue, hand them a new tool, then ask: "what can we get for you today?". Other complaints and negative behavior I'd just outright tell the customer with empathy "I know everyone has a lousy day, but I only get one day with you a week, so what can I get you?" Most of the time it works well and trains the customer that you're not there to complain to about personal issues, but to do business with. Sometimes a customer just needs to vent, and by all means, vent away, then let's do business.

Our goal is to sell all the time. Sales feed collections by getting the customer to pay more or having them open a credit account. Opening a credit account with the flagship credit company is a goal for you as a dealer. The truck accounts feed the credit accounts when purchases are too large to be held on the truck account. When you complete a credit agreement with the customer and the flagship credit company, you get paid that day or the next day. However, the flagship credit company doesn't pay you 100% of the sale; depending on that company's rules, they hold back 2% to 3% of the sale. That percentage is held in a reserve fund to help pay for any recourse loans that you've written.

Each flagship has different rules. The one I'm most experienced with is where they chargeback any non-payment account to the dealer that has written up that sales contract. The percentage they chargeback varies on the type of contract you've written with that non-paying customer. There are two basic chargeback types: the standard contract, which charges back 25% of the loan so all your profits get charged back to you, and a full-recourse loan, which charges the full loan back to the dealer who wrote the contract.

Standard chargeback customers need at least a decent credit rating to get that contract. For customers with a lower credit rating, the flagship company would do a full recourse loan. This means that anything the customer owed and didn't pay was charged back at the full amount. Knowing your credit rules is very important when going through your training with the flagship company. They won't want to tell you how common chargebacks are. In my decade on the tool truck, I usually averaged ten to fifteen new contracts and one chargeback a month, so 10% to 15%. When you do a lot of business, some of it will go bad; that's just part of the journey. The way it doesn't have a large impact on your bottom line is when you're constantly recharging that reserve account with the 2% to 3% on each sale. The program is set up to pay you out the reserves at the end of the year, but I never saw it because it was constantly drained with the bad debts it was covering.

Let's give you an example of how a credit sale of a toolbox affects your cash flow and profits. We have a customer named Joe, and he wants to get a toolbox because he's out of space for tools and likes the deal you're running. These larger purchases are usually provided by you as a dealer doing your job and viewing the customer's needs in the shop. Also, you give your customers the buying power to make these purchases by offering credit application programs. These programs can be set up either by you or by the flagship credit team.

At a minimum, you want every customer to update their credit information every six months to see how much they're eligible for. Fortunately, Joe qualifies for $7,000 with the flagship credit team. He wants to trade in his old box and get the larger one. Your deal on the truck is to get the box for $3,000 when you trade in your old box. This sounds like we have a deal, right? Well, yes and no; we need to look into the deal to determine if it's going to be profitable. To do this, we need to understand all the credit team policies. I'll be going by what the rules were in my business at the time, which can easily change over time or from one flagship company to another. So just replace the changes in the equation to figure out your total profit and exposure on this deal. The one major part, no matter what flagship company you're with, is if the customer doesn't pay, it's going to be a bad deal for everyone involved!

Let's say Joe doesn't pay a year from now or he falls on bad times. In this instance, a 25% chargeback will be applied to your tool bill account with the flagship company, which they apply to the tools you purchased that week. It first gets deducted out of the reverse account and when that account is dried up, a portion of the chargeback is added to your tool bill account each week. The account that's not paid is charged back prorated to Joe's account for the time the flagship credit team deems it a bad account, which is typically 120 days past due. Keep in mind that late charges and interest are being added to the account for those 120 days.

Back to the toolbox: this looks like a $3,000 total sale price plus tax of 8%, bringing the total to $3,240. You'll get the $3,240 credit to your tool bill account. If you had a $9,000 tool bill balance with the flagship company then the account would now be $5,760. Your profit and cost of goods are credited to the money owed, along with the sales tax. If you had a $1,600 payment for the tool bill this week to the flagship company, it would already be done with this toolbox contract. Now all the other money you collect on the truck accounts this week can simply be taken and deposited in your business account.

With an average margin of 30% on sales, Joe's $3,000 toolbox purchase gives you a gross profit of $900. Deduct the reserve 2%, on the low end, for the credit team, and the normal business operations of insurance, fuel, fees, etc., at 3%. None of this seems like a lot but it reduces your profit range from 30% to 25%. This is where the flagship company gets the 25% liability for the loan. It's beneficial to the company because it's an interest-bearing account that's paid the interest first. This is the account you're on the hook for until it's paid off. This is the best credit program that you can get from the flagship credit team; others are normally 100% full recourse loans and if they go bad, you're charged the entire loan minus any interest they made.

Then you ask "what happens if the dealer gets the toolbox back after Joe used it for a year?" Well, this box is going to be in a used condition, so as a dealer you have to give it a fair market value. Depending on factors like wear and tear, let's say the box is now worth $2,000 and Joe still owes $2,800 on the loan with interest and fees. The customer will get the $2,000 credit taken off his account, and now you'll be charged 75% of the $2,000 so you can resell the toolbox. This takes your chargeback from the 25% of $2,800 to 25% of $700 for the initial contract you wrote up with Joe. Now you have $700 charged back but a toolbox to sell. The toolbox will be recharged back to you at $1,500 on your tool bill (because the flagship credit company bills you 75% of the fair market value you have Joe's box.) I personally hated the system that the flagship company used because it benefited everyone except the hard-working dealer. Your break-even budget can't sell it for more than 75 cents on the dollar on what you gave Joe for the return, otherwise you can legally get yourself in a mess - if Joe finds out you sold it for $2,500, you'll owe him the $500 difference.

The flagship company calls it credit exposure. It's the overall amount of liability that your business has in credit contracts that you've written and co-signed for. I ran an average of $800,000 to $900,000 of total outstanding credit contracts. Keeping to the average liability on the 25% chargeback, I was liable for $200,000 to $250,000 if everyone stopped paying. The likelihood of the total non-payment of every customer is rare. These large numbers of exposure came from years of being a dealer and running the business as 70% dealer-financed and 30% flagship credit-financed. This also made me a ton of money because I kept writing contracts more than the rates of the non-paying customers. In my opinion, these credit risks and programs are necessary to pay off the business and make money, as well as controlling your tool bill. This is not meant to scare you from making credit sales, but to educate you on them.

Buying tools to replenish your inventory is a fine line to walk in the industry. The pressure from the flagship company will always be to buy, buy, buy because they're in the business of selling you more tools. You need to buy more tools to have a product to sell - it's hard to sell an item you don't have. Remembering that, you yourself might be a bit of a tool junkie also if you're getting into this business, but you're not a warehouse. The goal is to have a healthy amount of inventory for the customer to browse and decide on what you can provide to them, from the newest tools on the market to the specialty tool to get the job done. You're paying money to move your tool truck around, so make sure it's stocked properly. The balancing act of buying the proper amount is going to be a constant struggle. This ties directly to the tool bill, which is a weekly payment for tools purchased, and it needs to be paid. If this bill isn't paid, the shiny new tools from the flagship company stop coming very quickly, and this snowballs inside your business: it becomes impossible to order tools for customers or to transfer accounts or tools among dealers. The over-ordering of items that aren't selling eats profits, and the under-ordering of inventory kills sales. This skill is only learned with time, experience, and relationships with customers, local dealers, and your flagship reps to help balance it all out.

It's important that you know your flagship return policies. Suppose you get the newest, most expensive tool on the market and no one purchases it, or you have an old item that was on sale. What do you do with no moving inventory? Knowing your options with the flagship company is crucial, and not having the rules in writing can cost you a lot of time and money. The flagship company's policy can change frequently, for any number of reasons, but it comes down to the fact they won't lose any money on any return. In fact, this can cost you as the dealer quite a lot of money if you're not aware of what you're doing.

It's just not a simple dollar-for-dollar on returns. The variables are too high to have a program like that in place, so the flagship company has other policies. For example, if the items are worn then the company won't take them back at all, nor do they accept returns on certain items like a scan tool or certain type of electronic test equipment. The largest thorn in my side was the day that they enacted the lowest paid price return policy. This was a policy whereby they would only credit you the lowest price that you paid in a 365-day period, which we looked at in chapter two.

Warranty items are also returned. One of the biggest sales pitches of any tool brand is its warranty. You don't want to go into business with anyone that doesn't stand behind their products or tries to play games on warranty items. Customers buy products from you since you're there to warranty them. The Internet doesn't do this (as of yet, anyway). In my tool truck, I didn't question broken tools. I gave new tools with confidence, as long as it was within reason and I knew that my flagship company would warranty the tool. I wasn't going to give a guy a new toolbox because he had rust on it when it was sitting outside for years, but I would do that for any hand tools. Even if it was questionable, I would still give a customer a new product, to drive home the point that my service and reliability were strong with the customer. I would then hold those questionable items aside to review with the flagship rep later on. Later I found out that the flagship only questions you if your warranty levels are over 10% to 12% of your collection aid sales, although I'm sure this also varies between brands. Do not expect to be sending tools back that are not broken to get a refund.

The point here is to never really squawk about warranty items. Just ask the customer what their next purchase is and keep things moving. Of course, some items simply weren't covered or were out of the warranty period. This was common on air-powered tools or cordless power tools that needed to be sent in for repair. These repairs would cost money and were paid for by the customer. This is another training of the customer, to get them to understand that repair items aren't added to the tool account bill like a product purchased from the truck. Will it kill you to add it to their truck account? No, but it'll mess with your cash flow and profitability. What seems like only happening a couple of times adds up really quickly when you're trying to pay all your bills associated with the business. Having the knowledge of how your flagship bills you for repairs impacts how you should bill the customer for the repair. The way it always went down in my business was I issued bills on the day that the tool was received for repair, so I would bill the day the customer took possession of the tool. I would explain to the customer, before even sending the item in, that the charge would be paid in full to receive it back, and asking for 50% upfront to help offset the full payment when received back. Be warned that the customer won't be happy about paying for the repair plus his normal payment for the tools that week. Therefore, getting that money down will help you out and not push back your turn of cashflow per week for your business to operate correctly.

The flagship companies set the business up to operate on a weekly basis, so you must handle your own bills and the customers on a weekly basis, too. This makes a fifty-two-week year go very quickly if planned out in the correct manner. This can be done by the flagship company and they should have at least a three-month spread on your future orders. You need to sit back once a month to review your future sales goals and to plot a plan to hit those goals. I always had my break-even number in the back of my head, but I wasn't there to break even. I was there to profit as much as I could. This is accomplished by your monthly planning, even though the flagship company I was with was notorious for not getting the product to me when it was expected to arrive. This always made it interesting; I just had to adapt to the way I assembled promotions.

In the next chapter, we'll go into those parts of the business.

Chapter Nine

Sales and Collections Strategies

IN THIS CHAPTER, I'M going to share some of the most successful strategies that I used in my business. Is it the best? Well, for me, it required a load of trials and lots of errors. The amount of time spent tweaking different programs reached almost 100,000 hours. That's almost eleven and a half years, and even then, there was more to learn. There are always ways to make improvements.

I spent countless hours researching, reading, and listening to anything to advance my skills in sales and collections. The classes I took and the speakers I paid to see were all worth the time and money spent to acquire that knowledge. A wealth of knowledge is out there, and it is so deep and dense that you can spend the rest of your days trying to take it all in. Just taking the time to comprehend the knowledge then applying it, along with the multiple things going on inside the business and your life, takes that grit we spoke about at the beginning of this book.

We have a business to run, so I'll give you what worked for me. I'm going to tell you the best customer training techniques, sales development, and collection strategies that actually made me money. This isn't exhaustive; you should be learning from others and constantly adding more knowledge to your repertoire. The resources are there and I always had them in front of me, which forced me to learn them. The audiobooks or audio lessons to play whenever I had a moment to listen, like driving, walking, or bike riding. The books on the nightstand or in the bathroom to pick up instead of browsing social media on my cell phone. My home is littered with sales books and technology magazines. This forces you to take the time to pick up this knowledge and get it in your head. That, above all the rest, is the decision you need to make. The decision to take the time to learn and advance your skills is the game-changer for this business.

With that, I can give you my sales advice and experience. The first thing to know is who your customer is. This takes a long time to learn, but once it is learned, time and money will increase in your favor dramatically. The impact is so profound that it's the first skill you need to learn, before any other when it comes to sales. I hope you recall that this business is relationship-driven, and knowing the characteristics of the customer you have in front of you will serve you well. Judge the customer relationship while not judging them as a person. By looking at their actions with you over time, you can get a good indication of how they'll continue to do business with you. Simply put, if they were a hard customer to deal with in the past, then most likely they're going to be difficult in the future. The same goes for the good customers and, hopefully, you can grow the business with more of them.

I've had customers I'd never met come onto the truck (known as walk-on customers). These customers didn't even work at the stops I had on the route. They would come to warranty their broken tools or purchase something. The way I dealt with them was the same as any other customer: with a greeting and introduction of who I am. I always took care of whatever they came in for. I learned to never judge a book by its cover, as some of the least obvious people became my best customers.

I had a guy come onto the truck about two years into the business and he looked rough, to say the least. He weighed over four hundred pounds, smelled like he hadn't bathed in months, and slurred his speech so badly I thought he was drunk. The guy picked out $2,500 in tools he wanted to purchase. I told him the total and thought to myself "this guy is quickly going to backpedal out of here and not buy a thing." This is a normal occurrence for someone not used to premium tool prices; they're used to the cheap tool depot prices and quickly get scared of the pricing. Not him, though. He dug down in his gym shorts, pulled out a huge wad of cash and proceeded to pay me in full.

I ended up running into the same guy a couple of weeks later when he came back out to the truck. My gut told me that he had buyer's remorse and wanted a refund, but I was wrong this time, too. Instead, he picked out a $500 set of wrenches to get a free bar stool promotion I was running that week. This continued over the following weeks, with purchases paid in full and me being really happy. Eventually, we got to talking and I learned he was a hobbyist that enjoyed working on his old projects in his retirement. He enjoyed the products I sold to him very much and had the extra capital to spend on other items he enjoyed. He invited me over to check out his projects and tool setup after work. Of course, this gentleman at the time had spent thousands of dollars with me. I felt obliged and went to his home, which was out of character for me; the fear of being robbed meant I didn't normally go to customers' homes. During the visit, I found out he was an investment broker and had a stroke in his retirement, which was just one part of his health falling apart over the years. Working on his projects made him happy and seemed to refocus his life. We kept up a professional relationship, and I even extended him credit for the term of my business. The truck credit I gave him was to lessen the blow of some toolboxes he wanted to purchase. I was pretty sure he could have paid them in full, but wanting to have a tool account gave him a reason to have weekly interaction with the truck. At $200 a week and never missing a payment, he was golden to me and the business. He eventually moved to Texas, but he still called a few times a month to get the deals and I would ship him the tools. Giving him the tool truck credit extended our relationship to even work out of state, making it profitable above normal conditions. It's not uncommon to lose good customers when you or they move. Life happens. Getting good customers to stay is difficult and may not work each time.

Now, I'm not suggesting that you shouldn't be cautious about people. My experience with this man isn't common, but it can happen and the lesson is not to brush someone off prematurely. On the very same note, I judged each new person that entered my business, not only for their character but for safety as well. The fact is that tool trucks do get robbed, and you'd better know your surroundings. I was never robbed by gunpoint or force on the truck, but I've heard my fair share of stories. Keep to the basics of going to your scheduled stops where people know you and expect you to be, and don't stop - on the side of the road or anywhere else - for people you don't know.

Speaking of new people, there'll be new hires at your stops and you'll need to make a judgment call on them. When they want to loan your money out for tools, getting paid back should be first on your mind. Over the years of learning and losing money on new hires, I instituted a sixty-day rule on the truck. This is where I simply told the customer that after sixty days of employment, they can open an account inside my business. Until then, everything was cash and carry.

I had one exception to this rule, which was when they already had a tool account from another dealer who could vouch for their good payment history. Whether the customer had the history or not with previous dealers, I always demanded the customer's information during that first dealing. The information was the legal name, residing address, active phone number, driver's license number, social security number, and I would work into the conversation that we should be social media friends, also. This can seem intrusive, or harsh to tell someone "no" when they want to buy tools from you, but this was the answer they would get unless they met all the criteria of my background check. If you don't follow through with this for every single customer, it'll bite you in the pocketbook. Not getting the customer's entire history and contact information on the books cost me over $250,000 in bad debt over the years. Please reread that last sentence. A quarter of a million dollars. That's why the check is so important, and will help that number be significantly lower for you.

I would also ask to do a credit review with the new customer, and that would earn them a free hat or T-shirt. I presented this enthusiastically to give them the $10 to $12 item for "being a new customer" but what I was actually doing was checking their credit history with the flagship credit company. Bad credit doesn't mean a bad customer, it just means they're limited on what they can purchase from you. If you can't use the flagship credit to make large purchases, then you'll have to use your money to finance that individual. In the simplest possible terms, my advice is this: if the customer can't purchase the item with their money, then don't let them purchase it with your money. When it comes down to large amounts, let's say $2,000, if they can't afford to have that paid off in two months, then just don't do the deal. The risk and reward side of loaning money needs to be liberal to make the business prosper, but it needs to be done with restraint. Don't be blinded by the reward of a sale; all the aspects of the deal need to be in line. The promises people will make you versus the reality of paying off the bill are very often extremely different, so don't fall into the trap of promises and wishes of people; it'll harm you in the long run.

Knowing and learning the customer purchase history and purchase power cuts down on the time you need to spend with them as an individual. Spending an extra ten to fifteen minutes with a customer that has the buying power for a new toolbox is so worth it, rather than spending that time with someone that doesn't have the ability to purchase the toolbox. If they did have the power to buy it with your money and you let them, then take into account that now you'll have to dedicate your time to getting payment from that customer. Your time during the operating hours of a business day is limited, and maximizing your time is the skill we spoke of previously. This is why it's so important to set up scheduled payments.

One type of customer that can steal your time away is what I call the "Seymours." The Seymours are just that: customers that always want to see more. They never get around to making a purchase. They love to eat your time and energy up and are completely oblivious to what they're doing to you and your business.

Similar to the Seymours are the "Bullmours." The Bullmours just want to come out to the truck and shoot the bull with you more and more, regardless of how many times you redirect the conversation back to the subject of tools. They, too, are time and energy sucks like the Seymours, but instead of asking questions, they tell you how crappy their life is or how much they hate someone or something.

Then you have the "Freddy Mour." He is the most brazen bunch of the group, the freeloading Freddy always asking for free things. He likes to come onto the truck and ask for free items all the time, no matter what it is, and it's never enough for him.

All of the Mours need to be dealt with effectively and as quickly as possible, with the same formula you use with all of your customers. This is just the training of the customer that you need to do because they're stealing your time and energy, even if they don't understand it. Being upfront and direct with this type of customer is the most effective manner. Simply saying in a polite and strong tone, "that is all the time I have today, and business calls, so I must be going." Then I like to reiterate to them what exactly they're doing to me with "Thank you for your time and let me know your next tool investment" with a handshake and pat on the back directing them to the door.

The next group is the most difficult group to deal with, at least for me. The ones who have no intention of making good on their payment. This customer has all the red flags that they're going to be a problem. The reason this is so hard is that this customer is the most seductive, with those promises we talked about before. These customers make your job so easy and make it seem like collecting your money will be a cakewalk. The truth couldn't be any further. It's sometimes hard to see the forest for the trees, as some say, but the background check and sixty-day waiting period for financing will take out a lot of worries. Looking at the customer's credit score gives you a hint of past issues that can easily repeat themselves with you. The complete history makes the customer rethink ripping you off because you know all their information. The sixty-day wait weeds out a lot of guys that are here today and gone tomorrow. The big one to take into account is your gut feeling. This is a tricky one because more times than not I've been tricked by my gut because of that seduction of the sale. The business is founded to make sales, and these people want to do just that. So, your gut might say "yeah, sell!" but your brain and logic are saying "hell NO!" The saying that rings true still to this day in the tool truck world is "the easier it is to sell the item to a person, the harder it will be to collect it from them." The only combative way to deal with it is by making yourself have the ability to say no when the fail-safes you set up in the business aren't met. You can use the excuse that this is a corporate standard for the tool trucks, and apologize if that makes you feel better. The outcome is going to have to be the same either way.

This brings up the fact that the customers don't understand that this is a franchise, not a corporate store. This is a very common misunderstanding about tool trucks, the belief that I'm an employee of the flagship company. The customer needs to be educated that I'm not an employee and I purchased everything on the truck for resale. Some of my favorite quotes are "You get this for free, so why not give it to me?" The customer is ignorant, not stupid; you simply need to train them on the truth that this is a local business owned by you and managed by you. This can be driven home by a sign on the truck that it's locally owned and operated by yours truly. My other favorite quote is "Your markup is so high you can never lose." With this book and your help, the end customer will realize what this business is about. You must explain that the profits aren't so great that you have no worries, but instead, you have all the worries and little leverage other than doing what's right to the customer, accepting the same in return. The belief of many customers is that the flagship company will come to your rescue if need be, which is another fallacy. The flagship company won't lift a finger to collect your money or reimburse you in any way if your accounts go uncollectable. This won't be taught in any class but you can learn it here, so protect your assets.

You protect your assets by knowing your customer and having a pre-screening process that you perform when meeting them. You then further enhance those by building the customer relationship. Some basic sales are completed by using the steps the flagship company will give you on how they want you to perform a stop. This is a proven method that should be followed, and it goes like this:

1. Have a list of customers that you will see on that route for the day, complete with their name, phone number, the balance owed, payment history for the last five to eight weeks, needs, and backorder list of tools. The list needs to be printed and highlighted in different colors to identify the different tasks you need to perform with that customer today. For example, yellow highlight on the needs/backorder list for an item that was back-ordered for a customer, green on the balance for money due today, orange to follow-up with previous or future needed items such as a scanner or toolbox, and red if they're past due on payments. I would also circle the customers that are paid off or close to being paid off so I keep them on the books. This person becomes a targeted customer.

2. Enter each stop with a minimum of two tools that are either new or on promotion. You need to have the knowledge and ability to demo the tool, by showing its features and benefits. Show potential buyers how the tool will make their job easier. For example, by entering the shop with the knowledge of the fine-tooth ratchet design and how that decreases the arc swing of the ratchet. The smaller arc means that the ratchet needs less room to turn a fastener when stuck in a tight space. We know that everyone here has to work in a tight place in different jobs and taking out a demonstration prop to illustrate the use of the ratchet gives a visualization. This creates value for the customer and some perceived costs to obtain it.

3. Give the customer a reason to buy once you've created the value and perceived cost of the tool. This was my favorite part of the entire business because it involves using marketing skills along with some imagination. If you don't want to rely on the flagship company's promotions, you can build a sales promotion with your imagination and skill set.

4. After the demonstration, you take care of any other tool repairs or sales needs. This can be quickly accessed with the highlighted information on the list. Reset payment terms if a purchase is done, then collect your payments. I would also have a sales flyer that I wouldn't hand out until I gave out the receipts. The reason for this is to keep their attention on the tool demo or promotional pitch. Then, when they got the sales flyer, I'd often review it with the customer and explain the best deals.

These are the basic four steps taken with each and every customer you'll see that day. It'll get very repetitive and make you feel like it's Groundhog Day if you don't add your special flair into the mix. This is where your personality is going to make it fun, not just for the customer but for yourself, too. The temptation to not follow through with the steps is very high and easy to do. The list can get set aside and you tell yourself you'll just remember it all. Next, the tool demos stop, along with the sales promotions. Then you pretty much become a bill collector and a mobile warranty store. That's only going to hurt you.

Each business, no matter the industry, has a set process and any deviation will cause poor results. Inside my own business, I fell into the laziness trap of not doing price lists and slowing or halting tool demos. I could see the impact on my bottom line when I did this. Your motivation can go up and down with your emotions, but your process needs to stay consistent regardless.

The way I would stay the course or get myself back on the process is just reminding myself that it's the key to staying in business. I knew that avoiding it would end in failure or, at the very least, yield poorer results than I wanted. The way that I kept my motivation up for ten years was the sales promotion that I incorporated into my business. This was my outlet in the franchise to do what I wanted, to create something fun and profitable. With a little enthusiasm and effort, this will make you a success.

Let's go back to that ratchet demo example where we gave the features and benefits of the product, now let's slam it out of the park with a Reason to Buy Now . This is the reason that the customer wants to spend their hard-earned money with you. Maybe the features and benefits weren't quite enough to get the customer to commit to the investment. This is where we insert the sales promotion. When I walked into the stop to show off the new ratchet, I would also walk in with a five-gallon bucket with "trades" written in marker on the side. It would grab the customers' attention and pique their interest to find out why I had the bucket. After walking in and grabbing attention with the bucket, I would go into the features and benefits of the ratchet. Next, I would go into the sales promotion, explaining that, for a very limited time, I'm allowed to accept trade-ins, meaning I would take any old, beat up, ugly, even non-functional ratchet as a trade-in with a bonus of any brand type, too. With this trade-in type of deal, you'll receive a certain amount off the new ratchet. This is giving a story of the deal and a limited time on the deal, which are two things that appeal to almost everyone and can make a huge difference to your sales numbers. This is much better than giving a discounted price on the ratchet, because a limited trade-in deal makes the customer participate and feel like they got a great deal on the tool. Which would you feel better about: "Today I can get $25 off the ratchet price" or "For a limited time, I can get $25 for a broken tool sitting unused in my toolbox"?

The trade-in sales promotion can be used for everything and is common on larger items, too. The tool trade allowance, or TTA, is the amount of discount you can give while still making an average 30% profit. When you get an item from the flagship company, they have the list price for what it retails at and the Discount List Price, or sales price, and the difference is the TTA. If the ratchet had $25 trade-in value, that can be used for sales promotions, which was given back to the customer with the trade-in.

All of these different sales promotions bring enjoyment to the customer and you can feel it when presenting it. Another sales promotion I enjoyed was running contests. This was so common in my business I limited it to eight to ten times a year, because I didn't want the customer to get burned out or overly familiar with the contests, making them unable to engage. It's easy to overdo contests because they're so effective. Whenever I did a back-to-back sales contest, it lost the luster, so I decided to space them out over the year. Each contest, on average, lasted two to four weeks with a prize at the end. If you think that you have to come up with ten different sales contest ideas, don't worry, you get my proven contests! Additionally, the flagship companies normally come up with a nationwide contest at least twice a year, if not more. I never turned down a flagship company contest plan; they have it thought out, with prizes included, it would be profitable. These contests from the flagship company will have you buying the product from them to sell. These "canned" contests come with enough product to cover a table or a toolbox on the truck.

Let's look at an example of a package deal of $10,000 list price from the flagship company. You get a TTA of 30%, making the discount list of the package $7,000. This gives you $3,000 of TTA on all the products in the package deal, and the flagship company sells you the prizes for the remainder $3000. For this example, they sell you a BBQ set for $1,000 as the grand prize and an additional $2,000 in other smaller prizes. The smaller prizes can be items like shirts, hats, coolers, etc. and these are won by lots of customers, while the grand prize is won by only one customer. This was always an easy canned contest from the flagship company.

One thing I didn't like about the canned contest was that you needed to sell every item to make the contest work in your favor. And sometimes the prizes weren't the quality I'd expect, such as the $1,000 grill. That's why I'd set up my own contest with close to the same format, but it favored me instead of the flagship company. The way I would do this is by buying smart from the flagship company on items that are proven sellers. Each flagship company can give you the most commonly sold items to review, and with your knowledge of what sells on your route, you can make a good purchase of tools with good TTA. Then you will use roughly the same budget as the canned contest of $10,000 list ($7,000 at TTA). Remember, the flagship company's goal is to sell more tools to you. But instead of getting the canned prizes, we go out and get prizes in the $2,000 range. This gives us a $1,000 cushion in case some of our tools don't sell. Doing things this way will require some upfront cost from you as a dealer because you'll be buying the prizes outright. But the main thing to take away is that you're choosing the prizes and the total amount. This gives you the power to decide on what to get and it gives you wiggle room in case you don't sell all the items during the contest. These are the basics of the financial part of the sales contests. Now, how you set them up and market them is going to be very different.

One of my favorites was the envelope game, a popular sales contest that can be presented in different ways. This contest involves you taking a bunch of envelopes and writing a prize inside each one. Then you hang the envelopes up all over the inside of the truck. You also set out the prize items all over a toolbox or table to let the customer pick out the item they want or one that you showed. You give the customer the choice to pick an envelope, and he gets his prize instantly. Be smart and don't put all your top prizes out at once; mix them with a variety of the lower prizes. Making it fun is the only trick to this game. It gives every customer the free choice of picking the prize. Plus, I would always put in fun ones like "get a free hug and kiss from your tool dealer." It gets a good laugh and throws them a prize for humor.

The envelope is just one presentation. Sometimes I would swap the envelopes out for balloons, where they pop a balloon with a note on the inside. At Christmas time, do the same with ornaments that they break open to see the prize. This can be used with anything you imagine. The rules can also vary; you could try "buy one item, get one envelope" (or whatever object you use), "buy two items, get three envelopes." I also ran one where if the customer bought and paid off an item, they would get an extra envelope.

Sales contests can be very simple; in fact, the simpler the better. Explaining it forty-plus times a day for weeks gets mind-numbing. I had a fun and simple game called "the power of ten." It's a contest that only allows ten people to play, which creates urgency.

It goes like this: you pick out a larger promotional item that's intriguing enough to get the customers' attention and will also fit into your budget for the power of ten. Using the ratchet example, at $25 off I would get ten ratchets. Instead of discounting the ratchets or taking a trade-in on them, I would charge full price but give the customer a one-in-ten chance to win a prize. If your math is right, ten ratchets with $25 off each makes a $250 budget for a prize. The contest is made more interesting by choosing a $250 prize like a small tool cart, TV, bicycle, mini motorbike, rifle, or anything that'll interest your customer base. Then you get a card with ten lines on it, numbered one to ten, and it also has a scratch-off panel with one of the numbers underneath it. With the purchase of the ratchet, the customer gets to pick a number and you write their name beside that number. Once all ten ratchets are sold, the scratch-off number is revealed and that number wins the prize. This can be done using any number up to twenty (just rename the competition to 'power of twenty'), but it takes a lot longer to complete.

This isn't a hard contest, just a piece of paper, some effort on your part, and the upfront cost of the prize. Often, I would do this contest in a day or two along with other sales. This helps drive the sales up and provides more enjoyment to the customers.

A particular crowd-pleaser contest I ran was free money sales. This is a sales contest where you can change the rules to produce the desired results. For example, you can leverage the contest towards selling more products or collecting more money. One variation involves getting an empty water jug from those office style water coolers, tape over the hole and then put a slit into that tape so it looks like a coin slot. Next, get $250 in five-dollar bills, take that wad of cash and roll it up in a thick rubber band. It'll look like a big wad of cash, which you're going to walk around to each customer, along with the water jug. Walking into the shop with an empty water jug on your shoulder and a fat wad of cash in your pocket will grab attention from your customers. Everyone wants to know what's going on.

After you demo the product, you explain the water jug. I would do this like "I know you want to know why I have a water jug, and I also know something else about each and every one of you here." Then I'd pull out my wad of cash and watch their eyes go directly to it. Then I continue with "The thing I know about everyone here is you want some free money." Heads would shake and some even say it out loud: "Yes, I *want* money!" I replied: "So I'm here to give everyone the chance to win free money, just by simply taking whatever item we have on promo today. With each purchase of the item, I'll staple your name to this five-dollar bill and drop it in my water jug. When all the items are gone, we open it up and pull a name from the pile of bills. The winner will take all the cash-free and clear." Soon you'll be walking around with a jug full of money, and that grabs everyone's attention at the stop.

Again, this is editable for your needs. It can be payment driven or $1 bills, just as long as it fits into the prize budget. I generally had a minimum 1:2 ratio when giving out cash. I'll have $10 off an item in discount to give $5 in cash prizes, and that's my bare minimum. Most of the time it'll be at a higher ratio. The reason for that is some people won't pay you on time, or some will try not to pay at all. This is true for every contest. The reason I'm harder on cash prizes is because of the perceived value of other prizes. More than once, I used a mini motorbike that I bought for $250 online. Someone else will perceive that mini motorbike as $400 to $500, making them play more in the contest. The same exact thing can be said about a tool cart that you give away as a prize; it might retail for $500 but you paid only $350 for it.

You may think to just give away items that you sell because you get the best deal on them, right? From my experience, I find that has quite the opposite effect. It causes more issues later on. Just about every time I would give out a prize that came from my inventory, the customer would think it's okay to trade it in for a different color or ask for the cash instead. That results in having to tell them no, which can have a negative impact on the relationship.

The sales prop contests are games that the customer can play to win prizes or discounts on tools. The prop itself can be anything - a spinning wheel, a cornhole toss, a roulette wheel, even a Plinko board. They'll be crafted by you for whatever purpose you decide the game to be.

There are only two types of sales prop games: sales or collections. Using the "spin the wheel" game example for sales, the idea is when the customer purchases an item, they can spin the wheel for a prize. For collections, the customer gains a spin by paying extra on their account.

Collection games are common and you need to know what you're doing to make them effective and profitable. Remember, giving out a prize just for payment takes away from your bottom line - the customer already should be paying on time, but paying more than required will take some extra motivation. Different methods are used from payment cards where the customer makes a payment and gets a hole punched in a card just like a "free coffee or car wash after your tenth payment."

Most of the time I planned my collection games around the holidays and even when I wanted to go on vacation. One of my favorites was five-card poker, which I started three weeks before the holiday or vacation. Each week that I received payment, the customer would receive a card that they picked from a deck of cards. With three cards and three weeks gone, I'd be off for week four and return on week five. On week five, they had to either make up that missed payment or have the missing payment for week four already set up for automatic withdrawal in order to receive the cards for weeks four and five. I know this sounds silly, but it does work effectively. It may not always work, but at least you try to make it interesting and fun for them to do business with you. Once the customer has all five cards, you deal yourself five cards out of the deck and the best set of cards wins a prize. Alternatively, you can record all the cards from each customer, and then the best hand out of everyone wins a prize.

Collection games are as important as sales games because cash in hand is king in any business. Giving bonuses or the ability to play the game with a larger payment might seem like you're killing your accounts receivable, but looking at increasing your turn and getting the customer to replenish the account can be more valuable than collecting that extra 5% on a customer. The jacket program that the flagships run is a tricky collection contest, where they want you to give a jacket away if a customer has no missed payments over the cold winter holidays.

The sales and collections contests take time and energy plus some marketing skills. I have no background in either sales or marketing, so if I can make it happen, so can you. Now guzzle up your coffee and those energy drinks because it does require planning and extra hours. The reward will always be worth it; even if the event goes terribly and you break even with the prize money, your customers will appreciate the game and efforts, ultimately winning them over from the hundreds of choices they have to do business with. To me, it was like having your cake and eating it, too. Your customers are staying engaged with your business and your profits are coming in from it. So, I made the choice to always run fun and active promotions.

But what do you do when the customer has objections to the product or doesn't want to hear anything you're saying? It's going to happen daily, if not hourly, inside your business. Sometimes a customer objecting to a new product is actually a blessing; that the customer is even thinking about the product is the bonus you need to lean into. Rethink the objection not as a negative, but a communication barrier. The customer is objecting for a reason, so your job is to make them understand what they're really objecting to. No one wants to say "I don't understand this, please help me," and that's particularly true with the type of customers you'll have. So, you just need to simply rephrase the objection into a question to help you and the customer root out the true issue. We can use the most common objection, which will ring in your ears over and over again: "the price is too much!" This is also the easiest objection to overcome in my opinion. You're there providing a service to the customer that no one else is providing at that moment, visiting weekly to take payments on items, and repairing their tools. They might have your competitor also, but you're saying how much better and effective you do it, with the engagement in contests and other services like the training you help provide. When I heard the objection of the price being too much, the first rebuttal was "Compared to what?" then I just listen. Most of the time the comparison is against a Chinese import or the Internet, to which I ask if either of them show up here to deliver tools and take payments in person? That answer is always "no." Then I just simply sided with them and said "So you think the price is too much?" That triggers a "yes" from the customer, so then I'd ask the most important question: "Are you interested in the product?" What I'm doing here is breaking down and analyzing the customer's communication by directly asking their interest in the product. This is the answer that's going to tell me to move forward or just stop and move onto another product. With a solid "no" then it's time to move to another customer or product. If it's a "yes" then we break out my next favorite three F's. This isn't the Firm, Friendly, and Fair F's but another group I lived by in the sales role: Function, Fit, and Finance:

 Function: does the product function for your needs? Will it make your job and life easier?

 Fit: does the product fit into your life? Do you see the product fitting your life for your needs?

 Finance: is the product in your budget? Can we make the payments fit inside your budget?

 Some customers would come right out and say "yes I'm interested but the price is too much," jumping past the first two F's. Then I'd still go through the three F's, by reiterating them to the customer to build a foundation with them for this product and hearing the function of the product and how it will make their life and job easier. Then how it fits into their lives, making it easy to obtain and use. Last but not least, the final F, the finance part, which was the customer's objection. This is where we can circle back to what the customer is comparing this product to. When does a company like this come out to your work and demo a tool and then proceed to finance the tool with payments? For the most part, you'll be selling high-end products that have little comparison to a cheap tool that's in the box stores or online. This can be followed by saying "there is nothing wrong with cheaply made tools, hell I even own a few," then pause before adding, "but I just don't trust those tools to do the important jobs that I know you have to perform, Mr. Jones." Can you see how you're building value up to the customer? The equalizer is the business model that we'll offer financing on a weekly payment for the foreseeable future.

This tactic doesn't close 100% of sales, but it's an extremely effective method that I worked on for ten years.

The collections methods are the yin to the yang of sales. It doesn't matter how good you are at selling a product if you can't collect on it. This is the most cringe-worthy part of the business. Asking for your money seems simple, right? When you're face-to-face with a customer asking for a payment, you'd better be confident. The original three F's need to come out and play again (Firm, Friendly, and Fair). The reactions that you get from people vary vastly in each circumstance. They can range from joking and happy, to ready to hurt you with fists and swearing about your mother. One of my all-time favorites is when the customer tells you how they spent your money in Vegas or some wild bar-room brawl story. Now they can't pay you because of this.

Your ability to sell must match, or at least come close to, your ability to collect. I've seen great salesmen fail in this business due to their inability to collect. Keeping your collections in a format like your sales helps keep everything on track. Solid customer training with a routine on how you handle this part of the business is a paramount part of your success. This is done by keeping clear communications with the customer, with your three Fs.

This sounds easy enough when reading this, but in the field, it's a much more difficult task when you have a customer that clearly doesn't want to speak to you or get into it with you over money. To bypass all of the uncomfortable interactions and customer games people like to play when paying their bill, I just simply didn't allow it in my business. I'm not saying that they're never ever going to happen because, trust me, they will and they can be pretty brutal if you don't know how to handle it. To combat this, you need to control the communications from start to finish. So, that means when you first meet a customer or process their first sale and account, just simply state your expectations on how your business is run. The way I stated it was: "It's my job to come here and provide you with the best service and tools each week, to take care of any broken or worn-out tools. Your only job, Mr. Jones, is to pay me on time and the amount agreed upon." This is done by setting up a payment plan with options that the customer makes. One of the options I gave my customers was the date and time of when they wanted to run the card that they had on file with me. I would tell each and every one of my customers that "I give you the respect to pay me when it fits your paycheck schedule." This meant that if the customer got paid every two weeks, then I set up a payment on the day that they were paid for those two weeks of payments. If they had a $25 weekly payment then on the second week their card would run for $50. This can be set up even for monthly, but I don't recommend going over two weeks just in case a missed payment hits. It can get out of hand quickly. When a customer is set up to do a monthly payment and it doesn't go through, then you need to wait another month to get paid, so I preferred bi-weekly payments inside my business.

What do you do when the payments do go missing, or, even worse, when a customer goes missing? This is where the training and vetting of your customers plays a vital role. A customer missing several payments is a sign that your customer training and vetting programs need some work. Don't feel bad; in truth, they'll always need work and improvement. Whenever an issue arises, like missed payments, it falls directly onto you. All problems are your problems, even when it's someone else's malintent. As the famous phrase says, "the buck stops here," meaning the flagship company doesn't get involved with your truck accounts. The only thing you can fall back onto is your customer training program.

So, if we have a customer that can't or won't pay, your three F's come out in your attitude. As awful and uncomfortable as it's going to be, you must follow each and every customer through every time they can't or won't pay. This is a part of the training, having the same outcome and options given to the customer. This not only trains *the customer*, it trains *you* as well. Whenever I would get the objection of not making their payment, the customer usually tried to brush it off by saying "I'll just pay you double payment next week." Let me break it down for you: next week never comes, and neither does the double payment. This is an unacceptable answer for not paying your weekly bill. The chances of the customer actually following through with the plan of double that payment is under 5%. A knee-jerk reaction to the objection, and the rush that you'll always be in, is to say "okay cool, I'll catch you next week then, Mr. Jones." What you're actually communicating there is that it's okay not to pay you and you want to give your time and money away. One of the flagship mantras is "it's not okay not to pay," and it's very true because you can't afford it.

The issue is, how do you get results without coming off as a bill collector? Customer training! This is what I did each and every time to train the customer and myself. Keeping my three F's - fair, friendly, and firm - along with an open communications line with the customer by saying, "oh, I really can't do that" while making direct eye contact. Then I would follow-up with "I have to set up a payment today, or whenever your payment cycle is, so my business can function correctly." This is most likely going to have a rebuttal of "I just don't have the payment this week." Always treat the customer with empathy and ask, "why, what's going on?" Use a concerned, helping tone and look. Then ask "what I can do to help this situation?" This normally brings out the customer's excuse for not paying you. Repeat the excuse to them to justify it out loud and listen to their side of the issue. Trust me, you'll get a ton of heartbreaking excuses over time on why they can't pay.

Let's go back to an example we used earlier in the book, where Mr. Jones wanted to pay double next week:

You, after doing your demo and taking care of all the customers' needs: "Okay Mr. Jones, let's run your weekly payment."

Mr. Jones: "Sorry, I don't have it, I'll just double up next week."

You: "Oh, I'm sorry but I can't do that. I need to set up your payment today for my business to operate correctly."

Mr. Jones: "Well I'm broke and I don't have any money."

You: "I understand, what's going on? What can I do to help this situation?"

Mr. Jones: "My kids are sick and need new school uniforms."

You: "I get that the kids are sick and need new uniforms, and that's expensive, right?"

Mr. Jones: "Yeah, it's killing me."

You: "It's just that we had an agreement that makes your payment my paycheck, a paycheck that my business relies on to operate each week. What do you think the solution should be?" At this time the customer will be irritated and ready to end the conversation or come up with the double payment option. You listen to them, then come back with suggestions to get you paid the most amount now. "Is there a way that you can borrow the payment?" I love this one because most of the time they're disgusted with you even asking that, when they're doing the same thing to you. Most likely you will get told "no". That goes into the next question, "Can you do at least half of the payment today?" If you get another "no" then you need to restructure the payment plan. This is the last resort but a useful method. It starts out with "I know you want to double up next week," knowing in your head that's very unlikely. "How about instead of making you pay that large payment next week, why don't we just add your missed payment over time?"

Mr. Jones: "Sure, I guess that can work, but what do you mean?" They just want you to go at this point, but you need to persist because this is your business.

You: "So your payment is $50 a week, so let's just add an extra $10 bucks for five weeks?" said with a smile and a solution.

Most likely the customer will be happy not paying and the thought of not paying $100 next week, so they normally agree. Your business didn't get the payment but it did reset terms with the customer. The chance of keeping it at $60 after five weeks, because they just get used to paying that amount, is a lot higher than you might think. Using a calm, cool, friendly tone is needed to make this a successful interaction. Over time you'll become better and better at this; staying firm on getting the payment while staying fair is also your training as a dealer.

Now, what do you do if the customer doesn't want to pay because they're unhappy with the product or service? This is a pretty simple fix for you: remedy the issue there and then for the customer and show them that you're there for them. Even if they get pissed off and start yelling at you. Simply ask them what the issue is, and then fix it for them on the spot. If it can't be remedied there and then, make arrangements and assure the customer it'll be taken care of as soon as possible. If the item that they need to replace is out of stock and will be over a week to get, offer a truck credit or even a full refund. A hundred-dollar refund can give you a customer that pays you thousands a year. As one of my good friends always says, "Don't step over a dollar to pick up a penny."

The worst non-payment is the type where the customer disappears on you. They leave their employment and no one knows where they are. You can help curb some of that with relationships with the owners and other employees of the business. Most likely the owner will know some details on where their employee has gone. Plus, as almost everyone is on social media, it can also help to become friends with them on these platforms. In this line of work, it's also likely they'll run into another flagship dealer like yourself, which is another benefit to being in a franchise group.

How you handle missing customers is an important part of recovering any product or payments. Of course, I'm not talking about going secret spy stealth mode and tracking the customer's home (which some people do in this business). Actually, I have, in the past, gone to people's homes after hours to collect money. I must stress this, though: it's not worth it in any way, shape, or form. You can get into legal issues. I've run across this issue also where a runaway customer is at a new place of employment, not at my stop, and they threaten to call the police for harassment of that business.

You need to know what you are, which is a loan shark without teeth. Your teeth can be taking an individual to court over items he hasn't paid for. Ultimately it comes down to time and money: every minute you spend tracking down deadbeat customers is a minute lost with good paying customers. The result is no matter how you look at it, the most profitable way is to write it off and concentrate your time and efforts on the good customers. Another lesson is that when I did finally get in touch with the customer, on top of the time lost to tracking them down, they would never have anything close to the amount that they owed.

Remember that the vetting process is your first real line of defense against rip off customers. I would adopt the attitude that I'd rather have them do business with my competitor than steal from me.

My communication with the customer was always the same, with the three F's. This was in person, email, or over the phone. Mostly they don't want to speak to you at all. Either they're embarrassed by their behavior, or just want to skip out on the bill. The reason why they don't want to talk doesn't matter if they won't interact. One of the tricks I picked up over the years to get people to respond is with a phrase, a simple play on emotions and I would get a high percentage of replies from it:

Hey Mr. Customer,

It seems like you have given up on doing business together. I was hoping to continue working with you since we had a good relationship. We need to resolve some issues before they result in additional problems. How does that sound if we speak ASAP?

Humbly,

Mr. Tool Truck

This can be in text, email, letter, face-to-face, or over the phone. I found when you give the person the idea that they're losing out on something, like saying "it seems like you have given up," it makes them act now. Saying "we had a good relationship" makes it feel like it can still be a good relationship and that's exactly what you want as a tool dealer. The alternative is the threat of additional problems. No one wants additional problems, so that encourages them to reply also. You might be surprised at how quickly you receive a reply with this method. It took me years and many failed attempts at getting a reply, not counting the quarter-million dollars lost in the process. The phrase "you catch more bees with honey than with vinegar" could not ring truer.

In the business of collections, customers will make you experience the most anger you've felt in your life. So much so, you're ready to get into a physical altercation. The best level of effectiveness is the training that you give yourself. After you get the path to communication open with the customer, it's the only true way to get your business paid.

If you're lucky, and this is a common thing when going with a major flagship company, the customer simply shows up on another dealer's truck. When that happens, in my flagship company you get paid your cost of goods, which is 75% of the total owed. This takes away your profits and gives it to the current dealer servicing the customer. When the customer owes $100 and goes to another dealer, it gets transferred over to the dealer for $75. The customer still owes the $100 but the profits go to the current dealer doing the service. An odd thing I noticed over the years is that it equals out pretty close to even, meaning your transfers out just about equal the transfers in from other dealers.

    The things I have shared took me a decade to figure out, and I hope they fast-track you past the learning phase into the earning phase. Each part takes time to master and you'll always need to work on improving your technique. Keeping these sales and collections goals clear and written out gives you a leg up on the competition. Both parts are needed for the business to be a success. You're the piece that makes them thrive and it comes down to training yourself and the customer.

Chapter Ten

Growth Goals and the Exit Plan

IT'S ESSENTIAL TO HAVE a strong understanding of the business framework. This includes your support system of people in your life. We've already covered some details about the support group in your life earlier in the book, but in this section, I want to get into my growth in the business for over a decade.

These two things go hand in hand: support system and growth. Not only do I want to give thanks to my support system, but I attribute my entire success to it. I've received more help than I can count over the years and it touched every aspect of my life. As I've reminded you throughout this book, this business isn't a 9 to 5 job; treating it as such will put you financially in the red. As such, your support system is also a part of the business. It's the special sauce in the recipe for your growth.

Your growth over the years comes from you making the business a priority in your life. Without your family's understanding and support of this, you'll have impediments. There will also be times when they're required to sacrifice time or share the burden of stress. Having that support team behind you, with the proper expectations of what it takes to be successful, only adds the fuel to the engine.

I didn't know this when I first entered the business. I'd run my own business previously, but this franchise is a different animal. We didn't know the time requirements, and although it wasn't the sole reason, it ended up being the final nail in the coffin of my marriage and I got divorced. This is where I learned how important a support system is in your business, and how vital it is for growth. Different people entered my life over the next couple of years, but none could provide the necessary levels of support. They didn't understand the priority level of the business, and that it wasn't "just a job." Some people can leave the office, go home, and not think about work until the next day. In business, you can't do that. You work late, wake early, and often have dreams/ nightmares about the business.

It took me five years to find the right partner, and we give each other the support we each need. The system that we built helped me to hit my goals faster and more consistently.

The best analogy I can give is to imagine your business is a baby. You tend to it all the time, and the more care giver time it has - your support system - the more nurtured it can be. Without devoted parents, the baby won't learn and develop as quickly, and issues can arise. The same happens in business.

I was a single guy running the business for years, with on-again off-again women in my life trying to be that support for me. One of my big leaps was meeting the woman that became my now wife. Having a partner that understands what it takes to make success a priority makes a much bigger difference than you may think.

Unfortunately, not everyone is as keen to see you succeed. This became clear to me over time and was one of the inspirations for writing this book - not only to give thanks to my immediate family and wider support network, but also to be completely honest and transparent with you. The uncomfortable truth is that you need to choose who you have in your life. My grandfather had a phrase that has stuck with me: "If you lay down with a dog that has fleas, you'll come up with fleas yourself."

Cutting people out of your life isn't fun or easy, but if they're having a negative impact on you or your business then it might be the right thing to do. There are a lot of resources out there to help you do this, but the equation is simple: surround yourself with positive people that are moving ahead in the direction you want to go. The rest of the people need to be let go - as hard as it may be, it's better than getting fleas.

You'll be continually learning in this business, too. The responsibility is on you to do this; the flagship company won't force you. These days, the options are almost limitless: books, audiobooks, seminars, podcasts, online videos, business forums, mentors, and so on. Just get it done. You also must become an expert over time on the ever-changing products that you provide from the flagship company. You have to speak about them confidently.

The flagship companies will provide training on the product lines, but your job is to go above and beyond it. A good way of doing this is to look at what your competitors are offering, which is some simple online research. Knowing the difference between what you have and what the other guy has can result in a sale or leave you empty-handed. And don't underestimate the importance of using the products personally to understand the features and benefits. Ultimately, remember that you are the business, and investing in learning more skills is always a good thing.

Another aspect of growth is setting and achieving goals. Goals enable you to make your business the best it can be, a profit-center that your competitors fear. Without goals, you're running in a race with no mile markers or even a finish line. I would always have multiple goals, both in my personal life and in business, short and long term.

Goals can be flexible, to a point. Things change rapidly, so it's important to have some movement in your goal structure as long as you still move forward with them. A huge benefit of the flagship enterprise is you have peers operating the same exact business, so they're the perfect people to set goals with. Pick out the top guy and try to match or better him.

When I started, we had roughly thirty guys in the San Diego area. I identified who would be a good measure for what I was doing by looking at my break-even number - at the time it was $8,000 in sales each week - and then looked at the numbers of other dealers in the area, and made it my inspiration to do better than them.

At that time in the beginning of my career, I was ranked the seventh or eighth dealer in my area. All the while, I was watching and learning from the higher ranked guys, reviewing his sales and collection techniques. I always took the time to talk to the guys that were doing the numbers that I wanted to achieve, taking in their advice and leads. Most dealers in the industry will be happy to share their knowledge and wisdom with you. After all, having a larger group of dealers in your area doing well benefits everyone in that flagship company. It filters down to the customer directly, giving a positive perception of the company.

Now you've got all the information, education, training, and goals, in addition to your support team. The final thing you need is *persistence*. Everything else means nothing if you don't have that baseline of consistent action. Day in and day out. Motivation will vary, from all guns blazing to zero. Your success comes from your persistence. Without it, your career will probably be short, and this goes for any business venture you are going to pursue.

The next part is about a plan not to be confused with your skills and mindsets. Perhaps the one important part of any business plan is the exit plan. As I've mentioned before, the first question you should ask when you get into any business is "how do I get out?" or "what do I have planned for my exit from the business?"

We've gone into detail on how to get *into* the tool truck business and the huge benefits of it. But what about when you want to get *out* of the business?

We know that a key factor in owning a franchise is the marketability of the business. The same reasons that you got into the business are the same reasons someone else will want to get into it, too. These are the people that you can sell the business to when you decide it's time to hang up the keys.

Unlike other businesses, which are valued based on a calculation of earnings minus interest, taxes, depreciation, and amortization, the tool truck business is sold based on the value beyond the assets. The term for this is "goodwill" or "blue sky." If you can prove to a buyer that the business is worth more than the assets contained within it, then your franchise has goodwill. This is a downside for this type of business, compared to others that may have a valuation based on multiples of its revenue. Nonetheless, having a tool truck with a major flagship company means you've got a very marketable asset and you'll always have people trying to get into the business, plus it's easier for them to obtain finance through the flagship company than it is for people to finance many other types of business.

With that out of the way, how do you start with the exit plan? You begin by asking yourself some questions, like these:

1. What records do you need to have to show a prospective buyer about the operations of your business?
2. What does this look like financially?
3. Do you have a value on the business, and are you willing to negotiate?
4. Is it the right time in your life to sell?
5. Who can help you in this process?
6. What type of person can take over?
7. Do you have a sales strategy for selling?
8. Will you self-finance any part of the business?
9. Why are you selling?

Let's look at these in more detail:

What records do you need?

Your financial statements need to be ready for scrutiny, by your potential buyers and their accountants - and you better believe they'll be asking you about every perceived negative item. They include your tax records, profit and loss statements, balance sheets, and accurate customer lists. Having a strong set of records and a CPA will get you through most of those questions, but remember that the buyer wants to improve their bargaining power by finding faults in your records. Lazy bookkeeping only hurts you in the long term, and it's simply not worth it. Sloppy bookkeeping will make them wonder what else you aren't able to run properly, and will plant doubt in their mind.

Clean and tidy records also include customer accounts. Having customers on the books that haven't paid and who disappeared two years ago in your account receivable are sloppy errors. Those customers need to be kept in a bad debt column and shown to the buyer to prove that the business isn't perfect. The day you run across a tool truck with perfect books and no debt, run away as fast as possible. They're lying to you about the business. Honesty with a buyer builds trust with them, which facilitates your sale.

What does this look like financially?

Having your business plan in line with a good CPA helps with your tax implication for selling the business. Bear in mind that you most likely won't be selling the business for a profit. I know that sounds awful, but you have a depreciating asset with your truck, and the other parts of the business are the assets. On the positive side, not selling for a profit also means you aren't liable for capital gains tax.

Do you have a value on the business and will you negotiate?

This is the real talk and numbers for a buyer to look at. I've seen too many owners put a value on their business that's simply out of touch with reality and no one would be willing to pay it. As with real estate, the value is ultimately what someone is prepared to pay for it. You increase the odds of that by having a strong financial history to prove that the business makes money. No one wants to buy a failing business at a premium price.

A good way to calculate the value of your business is by looking at the cost of turning it back to the flagship company. That'll give you a baseline number, and the truth is the flagship company won't give you anywhere near what an outside buyer would pay. The flagship company I was with, for example, wouldn't buy accounts receivable - yet at one stage in my career, I had over $300,000 in accounts receivable. Outside buyers would be prepared to factor that into what they pay for the business.

This is where you need to negotiate based on your knowledge of the numbers. We know the three major parts of the business: the truck, inventory, and accounts receivable. What you also need to know is how the buyer will be financed. The truck itself is easy, as its fair market value can be readily found. The inventory is another hard number that you work out based on what the flagship company would pay if you sent it all back, minus any discounts, and you can take into account any restrictions the flagship company may have on how much inventory it'll lend to a new franchisee. If you do have more inventory than the flagship company will finance, and the buyer doesn't have enough capital to cover the cost, you can either sell the difference to accounts receivable or take the hit in the discount returns.

Before we move on, let's take a closer look at accounts receivable. This is the most negotiated part of any business sale. The flagship company I worked for would only finance accounts receivable when they had a qualified buyer, at a rate of 75% of the listed value. Accounts receivable are only as valid as the historical record they're set with, which again demonstrates the importance of strong record keeping. You'll need to explain to the buyer that 75% of the value is actually closer to 65% because you've already paid all the sales tax on the total of accounts receivable. Let's use an example of $100,000 in accounts receivable at the dealer list price. The flagship company will finance the new buyer $75,000 of that, and it's up to you to negotiate the difference.

Is this the right time to sell?

Ultimately this is up to you and your situation. I came out when I felt it was the right time financially and mentally. Talk to your support team, analyze the financials, weigh up the pros and cons. Do you want to retire completely? What will you do once you're out? How much money would you need? Spend some time thinking it over seriously before making a decision.

Who can help you and who could take over?

These two questions are interlinked. The selling of the business is done through the flagship company because the buyer will be representing them as the next owner. You can still get a business broker and list the business on the Internet, which will get more eyes on the business and increase your potential number of offers. The flagship company will also have candidates that have applied through their channels for becoming a franchisee, although they may not have a candidate for you specifically. When you're fielding potential buyers, make sure they're cleared with the flagship company too, which will ensure no one's time is wasted.

Will you self-finance any of the business to the new owner?

This comes into play once you know how much the flagship company will finance and what your numbers are. If the business is worth $250,000 and the flagship company will finance $170,000 then the buyer can either pay the $80,000 difference or you can offer to finance it for them on a term. My recommendation is to avoid personal financing wherever possible, as it'll be cleaner and mean less stress for you.

Why are you selling?

There are various reasons you may have for selling. For your own good, come up with the most logical and valid ones; this not only helps the buyer understand the reasoning, but also gives them a story about the business. This isn't a small purchase and buyers can smell dishonesty. There's no shame in selling for whatever your chosen reason is, and having a real and relatable reason can help to facilitate the deal.

Selling was emotional for me. I had put blood, sweat, and tears into my business for over a decade. I had to focus on keeping my emotions in check through the sale process and not let the small things put the brakes on the deal. The same methods you use to be successful with customers are the same ones you need when it comes to dealing with the buyer and remember to let the buyer know you want him to be successful in his new business.

In Closing

RUNNING A TOOL TRUCK business was an emotional time. I learned so much more than I ever expected, and the experiences I had can never be taken away from me. I hope I've shown you some of those in this book. With good and consistent service, you, too, will grow a loyal and reliable customer base that you can train - and they'll train you as well. Without them, it wouldn't have ever been a successful business.

I'm sure the question on your lips is "So, was it worth it?" It's hard to find an opportunity in life that allows you to control a $280,000 business for merely $26,000 initial investment. At the time, I had $80,000 to my name after selling my house and toys, and I had to live off the remaining money while I was building the business. I built that $280,000 business to produce over a million dollars a year in collected sales for several years. That might sound glamorous but it took a lot of time, a lot of mistakes, and a lot of hardships over the years. It was a hardcore business school that taught me in real time, on the job. The lessons weren't just in inventory, but customer management, negotiating, financing, business planning, marketing, training, sales, and a whole lot more.

The business required a lot from me, but it gave back more than it took.

Am I glad I did it? Yes.

Was it worth it? Absolutely.

To make a successful tool truck franchise business is to supply solutions to the customers. Not chasing twenties, but making the customer better off for doing business with you by making their life easier with your customer service, flexible payments, and knowledge of the products and supplying high-level products that make the customer money, save them time, and increase their quality of life.

The truth is that people don't care about your entrepreneurial goals to start a business. They care about what you can do for them. If you can't supply them with positive solutions for their problems then why would they pay you? You may love tools and have every piece of knowledge in the world about them, but this won't put food on your table. So, if you're getting into this business to chase twenties, save yourself some time and energy, and go get a 9-5 job. At least then you won't be on the hook for a $500,000 bill for the business. Passion is a necessity, but it's null and void if you can't supply a solution to the end-user. This journey will change you, and you can let it change you for the negative - I've seen it time and time again.

Or you can take control of it and take the negative lessons, turning them into positive learning experiences that you make the correct changes that grow your business and advance your life.

www.ingramcontent.com/pod-product-compliance
Lightning Source LLC
Chambersburg PA
CBHW070202100426
42743CB00013B/3015